More Than a
ountain
One Woman's Everest

More Than a
ountain

One Woman's Everest

TA Loeffler

CREATIVE PUBLISHERS

St. John's, Newfoundland and Labrador
2008

Canada Council   Conseil des Arts
for the Arts   du Canada

Newfoundland
Labrador

We gratefully acknowledge the financial support of the Canada Council for the Arts, the Government of Canada through the Book Publishing Industry Development Program (BPIDP), and the Government of Newfoundland and Labrador through the Department of Tourism, Culture and Recreation for our publishing program.

Cover Design by Todd Manning
Layout by Joanne Snook-Hann
Printed on acid-free paper

Published by
CREATIVE PUBLISHERS
an imprint of CREATIVE BOOK PUBLISHING
a Transcontinental Inc. associated company
P.O. Box 8660, Stn. A
St. John's, Newfoundland and Labrador A1B 3T7

Printed in Canada by:
TRANSCONTINENTAL INC.

Library and Archives Canada Cataloguing in Publication

Loeffler, T. A., 1965-
    More than a mountain : one woman's Everest / T.A. Loeffler.

ISBN 978-1897174-27-2

1. Loeffler, T. A., 1965-. 2. Everest, Mount (China and Nepal).
3. Mountaineering--Everest, Mount (China and Nepal).
4. Mountaineers--Newfoundland and Labrador--Biography.
I. Title.

GV199.92.L644A3 2008   796.522'092   C2008-900308-X

For all who dare to nurture dreams,

and those who helped pave my road to Everest.

Be careful what you water your dreams with. Water them with worry and fear and you will produce weeds that choke the life from your dream. Water them with optimism and solutions and you will cultivate success. Always be on the lookout for ways to turn a problem into an opportunity for success. Always be on the lookout for ways to nurture your dream.

—Lao Tzu

CONTENTS

Chapter 1

MY EVEREST

Every day is a journey, and the journey itself is home.
–Matsuo Basho

My Everest is not your Everest. Your Everest is not mine. We all have an Everest. Each of us. Sometimes the peak is literally Mount Everest, but most times it lies deep within us, figuratively occupying a mountainous inner space. It calls us to rise up, to do what we formerly labeled as impossible, and to be who we deeply and desperately want to be. I know that I have found an Everest when my soul furiously pokes me until I listen. Heeding this call to passionate adventure of any sort initiates a journey of intense, immense proportion that changes every molecule of my being. This is the story of my Everest.

JULY 2005

Signal Hill dominates St. John's. Its rugged slopes lift Cabot Tower to a perch of quiet splendour above the city, except when it is windy, which is practically all the time. The relentless wind whistles and howls and cuts with a ragged energy that begs to be harnessed. Tourists, seeking a connection with Guglielmo Marconi and his boundless view of the Atlantic, brave the bluster, hoping to catch a glimpse of a humpback's fountain breath or the icy turquoise of a grounded iceberg.

The CBC cameraman tried three locations before settling on the stairs leading down from the upper parking lot to the North Head trail. Garbed in mountaineering fare from head to boots, I stood across from Debbie Cooper, looking a bit overdressed for an outing on Signal Hill. Debbie, the anchor of the local evening news, explained that she would ask me some questions about my training, my climb of Denali, and what was next for me. My heart raced like the wind when I thought of my answer to the last question. "Will I actually tell her and all of her viewers?" I wondered.

I was freshly back from a thirty-five day climb of Mount McKinley. I refer to this massive mountain by its aboriginal name, Denali, translated as "The High One." Denali overshadows the surrounding peaks and tundra like no other mountain in Alaska. It towers 2,000 metres higher than its neighbors and actually makes its own weather. At 63 degrees latitude, with unceasing regularity, Denali delivers extreme storms and paralyzing cold to mountaineers. Its southern flanks are festooned with over 1,200 climbers a season, but the northern reaches on which we climbed were naked of all life but our own.

My face, carved in deep relief by Denali's harsh slopes, was weathered and sore. My pants drooped. My tired eyes scanned the vast horizon for the same views as the tourists who were trying to skirt around the huge camera blocking the trail. I could see the questions in their faces: *Who was this woman wearing big plastic boots and carrying a heavy pack talking to a news anchor on this July day? What did she do to gather this media attention?*

I had climbed Denali and stood atop North America at 6,193 metres. I was probably the first woman from Newfoundland to do so. Debbie called me back from the Atlantic and asked if I was ready to begin the interview. She reminded me to look at her and not the camera. As I hadn't given many television interviews I was nervous, but her first question set me at ease and I began to tell the story of climbing Denali.

The urge to climb had arisen like a tentative phoenix from the grievous pain of a significant relationship ending. In order to manage this enormous hurt, I needed something to throw my entire being into, and after a visit to Alaska, Denali poked at me until I knew. This was the challenge that would anchor me through the stormy waves of sorrow and anguish. I designed a physical and mental training program that would consume my life and leave little room for me to descend into the depression that lurked just outside the firelight of my soul.

Both the divorce and Denali would require me to exist in the world in new and fearsome ways. I needed my training to provide opportunities to practise standing on razor-sharp ridges and over deep, seemingly bottomless crevasses. A routine that demanded discipline and focus would give structure to the overwhelming emptiness that now permeated my life. Undertaking such rigorous physical training transformed both my body and mind in the ten months that preceded the Denali expedition.

Signal Hill was the focal point of my preparations. I hiked its trails, ran its roads, and reveled in getting to know it intimately. Given its significance in the climb, Debbie had chosen the perfect location for the interview. She asked, "Was there ever a time on Denali that you feared dying?"

I didn't share my first thought. I actually had feared dying more in the months leading up to the separation than I did on the mountain. On the mountain, however, there were three times when, if things had gone differently, I could easily have died. I answered Debbie's question by describing the descent off Karsten's Ridge.

"The snow conditions were awful. The snow balled up under our crampons giving us almost no traction. I was on a rope team with one of the weaker members of the expedition. He kept slipping and taking minor falls. We hadn't reached the lines we had fixed on the way up so we were dependent on the rope team's ability to arrest the fall if one of us slipped badly. The ridge dropped sharply 1,000 metres to either side. The consequences of falling were deadly. We inched our way down slowly, cringing each time a teammate's footing gave way. When the lead finally reached the fixed protection and we had some margin of safety once again, I breathed beyond the reaches of my upper lungs for the first time in hours."

Debbie then asked if I could say what the experience of climbing Denali meant to me. I paused to reflect and then replied, "For me, it wasn't actually about making it to the summit. Rather, it was about choosing the struggle, choosing to overcome, choosing the hard route, and choosing discomfort over comfort. It was about giving up preconceptions and preoccupations, building connections one experience at a time, and seeing the sunrise most every day. It was about knowing the wind direction and the weather both inside and out, about growth both at a glacier's pace and at torrents that would put most rivers to shame. It was about building determination and perseverance that will serve me for the rest of my life. It wasn't about reaching 20,320 feet on Denali, but being present in every moment of the adventure of getting there."

As the interview wound down, I knew the moment of decision would soon be upon me. Would I give voice to the dream that was so hesitantly and cautiously forming inside me? Would I dare bring it out into the light for everyone to see? Was I ready to publicly admit to what I was hoping to pursue? After a few more questions about Denali, Debbie finally asked the question. "What's next?" she asked innocently, having no idea of the maelstrom she had unleashed within me. I inhaled sharply and answered slowly.

"I want to climb Mount Everest. But the idea of fundraising the $60,000 to make such a climb possible is daunting and terrifying. Scarier than actually climbing the mountain."

MARCH 2007

Twenty months later, I stood before Debbie Cooper's camera once again, this time at MacDonald Drive Junior High School. The school was sponsoring my Everest send-off celebration. I was leaving for the expedition the next day. Six hundred students filed jubilantly into the gymnasium and lined the bleachers. This was the culmination of my mission to inspire the youth of Newfoundland and Labrador to become more physically active and to follow their dreams.

Little had I known the previous May, when Jacinta McGrath invited me up the Southern Shore to Stella Maris Academy in Trepassey, what would unfold in the ensuing months. Jacinta had been a student of mine in the physical education program at Memorial University of Newfoundland, and now she taught physical education herself. With a connection forged by backpacking together in the Grand Canyon, Jacinta had kept in touch during many of my ensuing adventures. Eleven summers of camp counseling gave me the skills to impart life lessons in an engaged and humourous way. I combined photographs, stories, and music to try to communicate to the students in Jacinta's school, the lessons that Denali had taught me. I spoke to 100 students that day, the first of thirty-two school visits, that would see me reach 10,000 youth before I boarded the plane to Nepal.

In order to metaphorically describe my sense of being poked by fledgling dreams, I hid a small plastic pufferfish in my jacket. I projected a picture of Denali on the screen and related what happened when I first saw it. I had secretly dreamed of climbing Denali for many years. In July 2004, when I saw the peak in its immense totality, I surrendered the dream instantly. The only thoughts in my mind were, "It's impossible. Too cold. Too high. Too hard. I can't." I returned home despondent and seemingly dreamless.

My inner pufferfish is a hardy beast, however, and it would not let me drop the dream so quickly. When I quieted enough to notice, I perceived the persistent prodding of its inflated spines poking me until I promised myself I would climb Denali. At this point in the talk, the hidden toy came to life bulging back and forth from my belly. Instantly the children's attention was rapt, and I brought the spiny critter into view explaining how we all have an inner pufferfish who clues us in when we ignore our dreams. I thrust the pufferfish back and forth towards them warning that if we don't listen to those first nudges, the pufferfish only gets bigger and keeps on urging us to reconsider. I reached for another, much larger pufferfish, and the children erupted in laughter.

At the end of the talk, Jacinta presented me with an unexpected financial contribution towards my Everest expedition as well as good luck cards decorated with construction paper mountains and wishes of "Aim high but be careful." Tears rimmed and threatened to spill as I saw the potential of reaching out and motivating youth in this way. Driving home, passing through the dawning green splendor of Salmonier Line, my "pufferfish" soul jabbed at me once again.

I had learned to listen to the inner voice that gives direction to my life, and I knew, in that moment, that I had a much bigger goal than just ascending the world's highest peak. I realized that I had climbed Denali solely for me, to ease my own suffering. As part of my Buddhist path, I had taken the Bodhisattva Vow a few months earlier. Having vowed to serve others, I sought places to bring this promise into practise. After the trip to Trepassey, I knew I had found a way. I would dedicate my Everest to the children of Newfoundland and Labrador, hoping to inspire them to follow their own dreams and to become more physically active.

Chapter 2

RETURNING TO NEPAL

There is no pain so great as the memory of joy in present grief.
–Aeschylus

After my second interview with Debbie Cooper, it was time to stop talking about scaling Everest. The time had finally come to go climb it. Having just barely survived the last few weeks of whirlwind activity, Judy poured me onto the plane in St. John's, and I was now feeling very alone. Judy had been a major supporter of mine during the previous twenty months of training and school visits. I met her just after returning from climbing Denali and I wasn't sure how I would have accomplished everything without her assistance.

The excitement of departure was giving way to a string of questions and doubts. Anxiety stuck to me like burrs to a prairie pant leg, and I found every excuse to feel inadequate. "Where did my confidence go?" I wondered, as I settled into my seat. "Is my body okay? Why do I feel so tired? Is something going on in my body? How will I get along with my teammates? Have I trained hard enough for this?" My mind peppered itself over and over again. Finally, feeling frustrated with the discursive diatribe, I said to myself, "Stop it! This is not being helpful. You're only making it worse."

Fourteen hours later, as I disembarked the plane in Frankfurt, I thought back to an article I read on the plane about happiness. It suggested avoiding comparisons to others especially if the comparison was intended to make me feel bad about myself. "Good advice," I thought, as I knew emotions would be high over the next few days. Transition had always been a big challenge for me, and I suspected that the next few days would be no exception.

I got out my journal and placed a check mark in a box on the first page. A few weeks back, I had drawn thirty-five boxes on that page in a five by seven grid. My plan was to tick a box every time I worried that I might be inadequate for the task of climbing Everest. By checking the boxes, I hoped to interrupt discouraging thought processes by not giving them a chance to take hold. My Buddhist mentor, Susan, suggested that such thoughts were like pigs in your house. If I have a hog in my home and I feed it, it will want to stay. If I starve the pig, it will eventually go in search of food elsewhere.

"I am okay. Every moment. I have worked hard for this and now I must avoid feeding any doubt. Plan my climb and climb my plan. Go gentle. Go with compassion. You know the first few days will feel long and hard. Find your place. You can do this," I said silently to myself, and found a quiet corner of the airport to practise some meditation.

Thirty-six hours after departing St. John's, I climbed down the airplane steps onto the runway at the Kathmandu airport. The thick morning air brushed my cheek and filled my nostrils with memories of past arrivals. Passengers scurried into the terminal and snaked their way through the dim halls to customs and baggage. I filled out my embarkation card and a shiver went through my body as I checked "Mountaineering Expedition" as my answer for "Purpose of Visit." I was arriving in Nepal to climb Mount Everest! Me–climbing Mount Everest–I could hardly believe it was actually happening. The swaying crowd moved me from my mental reverie and I spotted my two huge duffels across the baggage area. I loaded up a cart and steeled myself for the vibrating throng I knew would be waiting outside the airport doors.

Just past the glass doors, hundreds of people waited. Touts, taxi drivers, and family members kept their eyes firmly on the airport doors. I paused, steeled myself, and pushed my cart towards the teaming mass of humanity. Raj, a dear Nepali friend, leapt forward out of the crowd and placed the customary garland of cheerful orange flowers around my neck. "Phew," I thought. "Raj will get me through the crowd." We inched our way through, declining offer after offer of assistance with the bags. I pushed the cart behind Raj as he managed to carve a passage through the horde. Both Raj and I spotted the sign with my name on it at the same instant. A representative from Great Escapes Trekking was also at the airport to welcome me. Suddenly two young men grabbed my duffels and we headed for the parking area with Raj in tow. At the car, Raj placed a kata around my neck. Katas are given in Nepal at times of arrival and departure. We made a plan to meet later in Thamel and my new hosts took over welcoming me to Kathmandu.

Driving in from the airport, I had images of being the orb in a pinball game. The car darted from left to right to avoid pedestrians, goats, cows, and other cars. The driver used the horn to announce his presence as the car careened around corners, down impossibly narrow passageways, and generally defied gravity all the way to the hotel. It was as if all the instruments of an orchestra had started playing at once, but each performed a different piece of music, a cacophonous blend of sounds and movement. Kathmandu was "Beethoven's Fifth" played backwards to a jazz beat with a reggae chorus, a blue's funk and a hint of Indian Sitar. I realized that I had been to Kathmandu enough that this chaotic road scene seemed normal. Ang Jangbu Sherpa met me at the hotel. He runs Great Escape Trekking and was one of the leaders of the expedition. He laid out the schedule for me and collected my remaining expedition fees. After he left, I went up to my room to shower and settle in.

FEBRUARY 2002

Five years previously, I had made the same drive from the Kathmandu airport with my partner, Liz. We had just spent six months volunteering and traveling in Africa. We prearranged our hotel at the airport and had no idea where the taxi was taking us. Our hotel was in Chetripathi, the neighbourhood next to Thamel. Our first morning, we stepped out of the hotel to explore. We stopped at trekking agencies along the way because we wanted to make arrangements to hike the Annapurna circuit. At some point, we found our way to the main street of Thamel. A shop on a small side street caught our eye and we headed towards it. Beside that shop, a young Nepali man sat on the doorstep.

He introduced himself as Rajendra Dahal. We talked with him about trekking and we liked him instantly. After several cups of Nepali tea, we excused ourselves to have lunch at the restaurant next door. "I think this is the one. I think I want to trek with Raj's company," I said. Liz agreed and after lunch we gave Raj the good news. He introduced us to Dawa who would be our guide. We left for the trek a few days later.

I usually consider myself quite comfortable with heights, having spent much of my life climbing trees, roofs, rocks, and walls, but the road from Kathmandu to Besishar gave me pause. As we reached the pass that marked the transition from the Kathmandu Valley, the road serpentined below us at a height and proximity to the edge that was both dizzying and sobering. I was glad that the bus driver appeared to be middle-aged. I used the logic that to reach his age, he must have survived this drive often. On this road, if you didn't pass on a curve you would never pass, so the Nepalese have an ingenious system for intra-corner communication that involves much horn honking and the bus conductor thumping on the side of the bus. After offering a prayer for the bus's safe transit, I decided it was better not to glimpse at the valley floor thousands of metres below. Instead, I chose to stare intently at the seat in front of me for the next hour.

Six hours later we arrived safely in Besishar and followed Dawa to our teahouse for the night. The next morning, we began trekking towards Manang, the gateway to the Thorung La pass. Different parts of the trail housed people of different religions and ethnic groups. I found myself drawn to the villages that practised Buddhism. I learned to identify

Buddhist villages by the presence of mani walls, chortens, and prayer wheels. A mani wall holds stones into which prayers are carved, and a chorten is a structure that symbolizes the elements of water, sky, fire, space, and earth. Prayer wheels are round, metal cylinders embossed with prayers and when spun clockwise, send prayers heavenward.

As an experiential person, I enjoyed "doing" prayer by spinning the wheels. I was self-conscious at first, but I grew to love the sound of the turning prayer wheels. It was both a sound and a vibration, and it moved my spirit. It felt like a powerful way to pray. These same villages were also adorned with prayer flags of five colours: blue, white, red, yellow, and green, representing the same elements as chortens. When the wind furls the flags, the prayers printed on them are released. As we climbed higher into areas of snow, I loved the contrast of the brightly coloured flags against the brilliant white snow. I drank in the beauty of stark mountain faces pounding against the azure sky, while avalanches thundered down nearby slopes leaving clouds of white smoke in their wake, and the unmistakable clang and clamour of a rockfall sliding down.

Six days later, we arrived in Manang. After spending a day acclimatizing there, we headed for Thorung La pass. As we hiked towards the pass, Liz fell ill. She had a severe headache and began to have terrible diarrhea. We were not sure she could heal at those altitudes, so we decided to retrace our path back to Besishar rather than proceed over the pass. It was a big disappointment to give up the circuit, but I was pleased to have trekked to 4,500 metres and to have been surrounded by the peaks before the pass. As we headed back down, I realized that my cold had progressed to bronchitis, so I prescribed myself a course of antibiotics to stave off the infection.

Traveling back over the same trail enabled us to stay in different villages than on the way up and to truly appreciate our journey. It was tough having to explain to all the trekkers on their way up why we were going the "wrong" way, and I invented many flip answers that I would have liked to have given if I wasn't a nice Canadian. Back in Kathmandu, Raj welcomed us home and treated us as if we were his family. He made sure we were comfortably settled into our hotel, and we began to see Raj as our Nepali guardian angel.

Pleased with the service on our first trek, we arranged with Raj to trek with Dawa to Everest base camp. I could hardly contain my excitement. From the moment I learned to rock climb in high school, I dreamed of Everest. Mr. Hamilton, famous for his brusque manner, sponsored weekend trips to the Rocky Mountains. There, fearing every moment I would do something to anger Mr. Hamilton, I learned to climb, canoe, and backpack.

Our outdoor pursuits club spent the entire summer of 1982 climbing in the mountains and honing our skills. That fall, Laurie Skreslet became the first Canadian to summit Mount Everest. I was hooked! Four years later, I filled with pride and wonder when Sharon Wood became the first Canadian woman to surmount Everest. I never imagined I would walk in her footsteps.

After a week of rest, Dawa, Liz, and I flew to Lukla to begin our trek to Everest base camp. We retained our acclimatization from our previous trek, so we could proceed up quite quickly. We reached Kala Pattar in only eight days. It is a "small hill" of 5,545 metres that trekkers ascend to get a better view of Everest. Climbing Kala Pattar was hard work. Near the bottom, I could take 100 steps without stopping. In the middle, ten steps if I was lucky. Finally, at about 5,000 metres I hit my groove, felt strong, and could go twenty-five steps without having to stop and catch my breath. At times it was a mistake to look up and see the summit looming far ahead; other times it was like a beacon calling me ever upward. The reward was a view of 360 degrees of snowcapped wonder. Peaks I had heard of, and dreamed of, and read of for years unfolded in front of me. I peered down on Everest base camp, the Khumbu Icefall, and the long valley I had just spent seven days trekking up. I was in awe to be standing where so many of my heroes had stood. Looking across at Everest, I thought, "I could never climb that."

The wind was whipping the prayer flags on the summit into a prayerful frenzy so I stopped below the summit to take pictures and wait for Liz. We climbed the last fifty metres to the summit and posed for pictures before heading down quickly, as she was feeling the effects of the altitude. Altitude is a double-edged sword. It can give amazing clarity and solitude, and it can be cruel and unforgiving. Nights at altitude are harsh: the long darkness envelops me in doubt as I toss and turn, unable to sample the sweetness of restful slumber. Each bodyache, sensation, or moment is analyzed for the first sign of Acute Mountain Sickness (AMS). If I climb slowly, I can probably avoid serious AMS, but the doubt always lurks. The previous three nights had been very long and doubt descended like a heavy weight stealing sleep and warmth. Each day, the warm glow of sunrise on the white giants restored hope and balance.

By the time we returned to Kathmandu two weeks later, we had hiked 160 kilometres and climbed the equivalent of Everest twice. We experienced the Sherpa culture from the mid-hill elevations to the highest reaches of snow and ice. Dawa welcomed us into his home, and we met fellow travelers from around the world. Cards and reading played a big role in evening activities. I enjoyed the stories of the first Australian woman and the first

British woman to climb Everest. I read many other Everest stories over the next week because a Maoist strike pinned us in Kathmandu, unable to leave Thamel. I spent hours surfing the internet each day and stumbled upon Mount Kailash.

A sacred mountain, Kailash is regarded as the "heart of the world," the "axis mundi," and the center of Asia by Buddhists, Hindus, Jains, and Bons. For centuries, pilgrims have undertaken the arduous, and sometimes dangerous journey to Mount Kailash in order to gain merit and heighten their chances of reincarnation into a higher life. I knew in an instant that I needed and wanted to go to Mount Kailash. Liz agreed to come along, and Raj made the arrangements for the trip as soon as the Maoist ban lifted.

In choosing to travel to Far Western Tibet, we knew we would be facing rough roads, high altitude, and cold temperatures. We never imagined we would be stopped short of the mountain and that we would have to fight the Chinese government to be allowed to leave Tibet. We spent the better part of twelve hours each day as rodeo riders making our way from town to town, and trying to stay on the seats of the bucking and jerking land cruisers. At their best, the roads allowed us to travel sixty kilometres per hour. At their worst, we crawled along at ten kilometres an hour. Most roads fell into the latter category. Throw in a few landslides, precipices, river crossings, and high passes, and you have the average day of traveling in Tibet.

The sun often shone throughout our travel days. The solar radiation brightened moods and raised the temperature in the land cruiser to heat stroke levels, despite the bitter temperatures outside. Because of the dust, it was hard to open the windows for ventilation. By the end of the second day, I felt like a pork chop that had spent an eternity in a Shake and Bake commercial. When the temperatures plunged at night and snow began to fall on our tents, I felt like Shake and Bake leftovers that had been put in the freezer for the next time company comes.

We had two land cruisers in our group. One driver was a speed-loving, bump-smashing maniac, and the other was somewhat more cautious. Unfortunately, we rode with the first guy for the first two days of the trip. Because of some visa complications and other paperwork challenges, we had been off to a late start that day, and speeding was the norm. When we neared Peiku Tsu Lake, he launched us and the contents of our land cruiser into orbit, and Liz was injured, striking her face and ribs on the seat in front of her. We didn't realize the extent of her injuries for the next few days because it was hard to distinguish her symptoms from acute mountain sickness, and we kept hoping they would go away. When we realized that she was feeling no better, we decided to head down to a lower elevation.

At this point, we became acutely aware of the challenges of working within the confines of a Chinese group visa, having just one guide between two groups, and the remoteness of Tibet. To make a long, arduous, and frustrating story short, after thirty hours of driving, five hours on the border, and $100 dollars later, the Chinese government relented and let us leave the country. Raj and Dawa met us at the border and drove us to Kathmandu. Liz felt much better when we got to a lower elevation, and a visit to the doctor revealed that she had cracked a rib.

Although we didn't reach our goal of circumnavigating Mount Kailash, we had many amazing experiences while we were in Tibet. On a few nights, we camped near some nomads. For some, it was the first time they had seen Westerners. Tibetans have no "rules" against staring so they frequently would come up to us and watch every move. When we sat down to dinner, the kitchen tent was frequently unzipped by curious passers-by, and sometimes they would just peer though small openings in the tent. It was a bit unnerving at first, and we felt somewhat like caged animals at the zoo. Soon, though, we took to "when in Tibet do as the Tibetans" so we began to stare back and even got ourselves invited into one of their tents.

Liz and I followed the seventy-year-old matriarch to her tent. Its walls were dark brown and woven of yak wool. It was octagonal in shape and staked out with many guy lines against the incessant Tibetan wind. It was possible for a short person to stand upright in the tent, but those over five-foot-four would have to stoop. A long rectangular slit in the roof allowed the heavy sweet smoke of the dung fire to rise from the tent. One wall of the tent was dedicated to an altar to Buddha. It was festooned with small prayer flags and small metal bowls for offerings. We sat on low benches three inches off the floor that double as beds at night. We shared some beaten rice, but made our exit before the rancid yak butter tea was served.

Driving into Saga, there was no room at the inn so our guide arranged for us to sleep in the kitchen of a Tibetan guesthouse. We didn't mind as we had been bouncing around in the land cruisers for twelve hours and were just glad to stop playing gyroscope. There were only five narrow benches for six people, so, as the youngest, I volunteered for the floor. Fortunately, a mattress covered with yak-skin topped the dirt floor, since it was used for spitting, blowing noses, and general disposal. I added my self-inflating Thermarest mattress and sleeping bag, and I thought I had the best bed in the house. So did the duck.

Yes, the kitchen came with its own duck. Since I had fed her the leftover bread from our dinner, she imprinted on me and claimed me as her own. The term ugly duckling would be too kind for her, though her warm and welcoming spirit shone though her beauty challenges. She was a truck-stop duck decorated by broken white feathers with uneven black splotches on her back. She carried an overall cast of grayish-brown from her dusty environs, and it was hard to call her feet orange. She had no pond and little opportunity to preen. I called her Alice.

At some point during the night, I awoke to a warm heaviness on my hip. Puzzled at first in my sleepy state, I shifted and my load suddenly quacked. Despite duck clumsiness, Alice had the soul of a lap cat and, thus, spent the night on the TA treadmill. As I turned, she rotated from hip to back to belly to the other hip. The next morning Alice found herself, despite clipped wings, flying across the room when I found the four fecal packages she graciously left on my sleeping bag overnight.

OCTOBER 2005

Three years later, the autumn after I climbed Denali, I returned to Tibet. After the expedition, I had taken it slow; enjoying much needed free time after a year of hard training. When I finished teaching that summer, I realized that I was still looking for something–though I had no idea what it was. I vaguely knew that I wanted to make peace with going uphill and I needed to surrender to moving slowly, to breathing hard, to learning to enjoy the hillside as much as the summit, to staying present in each moment, and to embrace suffering without trying to change it.

When in Tibet the first time, I fell deeply in love with prayer flags. In Tibetan Buddhist regions, prayer flags fly from mountain passes and summits, from bridges, from homes, and from stupas and chortens. I fly them from my house and in my office at work; they reach a deep part of me beyond words. The Tibetan term Lung Ta literally means windhorse, and it has become practically synonymous with the English term "prayer flag." Friends had helped me finance the trip by pre-buying strings of prayer flags.

After my previous trip with Liz traveling solely by land cruiser, I longed to roam immersed and unprotected in the Tibetan landscape. This time, I chose to ride a bike from Lhasa, Tibet to Kathmandu, Nepal. The 1,200-kilometer journey crossed eight mountain passes ranging from 4,300 to 5,200 metres above sea level. On my website, I called the trip "Looking for Windhorse" because I was searching for the clarity that only intense physical exertion in high mountain environments brings me. When my life is simplified to the bare essentials of breathing, moving, eating, and sleeping, my mind, in turn, simplifies and I experience moments of vision, luminosity, clarity, and direction. These moments are fleeting and demand a high price, but there is such great joy and adventure to be found in searching for them. I followed an intuitive inkling that I would find such instances on the high passes of Tibet beneath the prayer flags that fly there.

The group for the trip met in Kathmandu for three days and then we flew to Lhasa. The plane flew directly over the Himalayas, and at one point a great excitement arose amongst the passengers. Mount Everest was visible on the left side of the plane. I managed to find a seat and stared out over the clouds to the summit of Everest and Lhotse. I aimed my camera and captured the peaks framed by the airplane wing. A shudder passed through my body when I realized we were flying lower than the highest spot on earth. "Could I ever stand there?" I asked myself. "No, probably not," was my simple answer.

After arriving in Lhasa, we had lunch at a restaurant owned by the Tibetan Mountaineering Association. As the walls were decorated with many expedition posters, dreams of high mountains sprouted alongside the fried veggie noodles that were my lunch. I needed to do some creative problem solving, as the rental bike that was assigned to me was more suited to someone six foot two inches rather than my five foot three inch frame. After considering many options, one of the tallest group members took my rental bike, the Nepali guide took his bike, and I rode the guide's bike.

The Potala Palace is one of the most recognizable buildings in the world. It was truly hard to grasp how large the Potala is until we exited, and remembered our inner tour route, and realized how little of the place we actually saw. The view from atop the Potala Palace was stunning. We began a gradual clockwise descent into the Palace, visiting rooms, chapels, and halls along the way. We saw the Fourteenth Dalai Lama's learning and sleeping room as well as his absentee throne. We also saw the shrines to the many previous Dalai Lamas who are interned in the Palace. The shrines could easily take your breath away, as they were each covered in 3,500 kilograms of gold leaf and each contained over 10,000 precious stones. No one could give me an exact count, but I think I must have seen over 10,000 images of Buddha in the Palace. Although the corridors were filled with pilgrims and tourists, the Potala was an empty place. It seemed lacking in spirit, and, much of the time, it felt like a dusty old museum. I left it feeling overwhelmed, sad, amazed, moved, and probably several other emotions.

Leaving Lhasa, we wove in and around and through traffic, passing the Potala on the way out of town. The first day was entirely on pavement, but the ninety-eight kilometres took their toll. We were treated to some lovely views of agricultural villages and met a French Canadian couple who had been biking for four months from Mongolia. The second day began with

twenty-four kilometres of uphill riding to the 4,700 metres Kalo Pass. It
took much willpower to pedal all the way up, though it was worth it
because I was rewarded with spectacular views of one of Tibet's most
sacred lakes. Its turquoise colour was breathtaking. At the top, all of the
tourists wanted to take pictures with me; they were amazed that someone
had cycled to the top. A rapid descent brought me to lunch and a lovely
afternoon's cycle along the lakeshore.

Day Three brought us our first dirt roads and took us up and over the
Karo Pass. We weren't supposed to cross the 5,050 metre pass until the
next day, but a climbing expedition had our camping spot so up and over
we went. It was a serious grunt and most in the group wanted to quit the
whole trip. At the pass, I did a form of Buddhist push-ups called prostrations for Susan. As I sprawled on the ground breathless after a few
attempts, I hoped Susan was having better luck with her prostration practice back in St. John's. The descent was wild, with several kilometres of
washboard road to shake my very core. Our fourth pass waited the next
day. We climbed Simi Pass (4,300 metres) and then descended forty kilometres of dirt road to Gyanste, arriving sweaty, dirty, and appreciating
warm showers.

Tibet days were blistering hot and the nights bitterly cold. We awoke
each morning before dark in below freezing temperatures, and if we began
to cycle before the sun hit us, we had some serious wind chill issues to con-
tend with. As the sun came out, it initially warmed us, and we worshipped
the sol goddess. But, like on Denali, the intense UV rays present at high
altitude soon caused us to call the sun the "death star," as it fried our skin
and lips. Despite layers of sunscreen and lip balm, I developed seven cold
sores and lips that would glue themselves shut at night because of bleeding.

Once we left Shigatse, we said goodbye to pavement until we reached
the Nepal border. The road surfaces ranged from pretty decent gravel
roads to the most sorry excuses for dirt tracks through the mountains:
rough, rocky washboards that took an intense toil on both bodies and
bikes. One pass stands out in my mind. Rather than Gyatso Pass, we
ended up calling it "Construction Pass" because it lingered in our minds
as the worst and most punishing biking we did in Tibet. It was thirty-eight
kilometres of riding uphill through the dustiest, roughest, and most broken
pieces of dirt road. We gained 1,200 metres to finally top out at 5,200
metres. We wore white dust masks, but they quickly turned the lovely
beige shade of the road. Since we were climbing the pass with 42 percent
less oxygen than at sea level, breathing through a dirty mask became a

suffocating experience. Reaching the top was a true joy, and the resultant views of the Himalayas were spectacular and worth every one of the 30,000 pedal cranks it took to get there.

The Tibetan Plateau muted my senses. Its colour palette draws most strongly from the autumn family of ochres, tans, beiges, browns, but there are also the most intense sky and water blues imaginable. Other than blue, there were no bright colours. The hills and mountains mix these tones in blankets and weaves that inspire thoughts of the southwestern United States. There were not many sounds on the plateau except the intense wind, the grinding of tires on stones, the bleating of livestock, and the voices of hundreds of children calling, "Hello." No birds sang. No bugs buzzed. There was only the relentless rhythm of breath going in and out as we pedaled against the altitude.

Two more 5,000 metre climbs delivered a magnificent view. As I rounded the last punishing corner, the north face of Mount Everest was abruptly revealed. Despite the challenge of getting my bike moving again at that elevation, I stopped and stared at the massive mountain. Different from the view of Everest in Nepal, here it was easy to grasp its magnificent stature. We camped at the Rongbuk Monastery and I often stared at Everest. The next day we watched a climbing expedition make their way towards base camp. We followed in a cart pulled by a high altitude pony. Arriving an hour later at base camp, I had an inkling that my inner voice was getting ready to speak. Despite it appearing as an impossible task to me, I began to contemplate climbing Everest. To seal the moment in my memory, I had a friend take a picture of me at base camp holding the Newfoundland flag. I nurtured a tentative thought: "This might be what I came to Tibet to find."

After leaving base camp and climbing the last three passes, we began the "World's Longest Downhill." After thirteen days of very hard riding, we all expected the descent to be easy. Expectations are so dangerous. After flying down the first 2,000 metres, we hit a very gradual descent gradient and were slammed by the most viciously cruel headwinds. I had to fight to go downhill, pedaling as hard to go down as I had the previous day to go up. "This isn't fair," I cried out at the wind. The group crawled and beat its way down for the next forty kilometres, bemoaning our fate over lunch. After a quick visit to Miralepa's Cave, we finally made it to Nyalam where the true, thrilling descent could begin.

After Nyalam, the road plunged 2,000 metres through the most magical gorge. The road, carved out of the sides of the gorge, was decorated with lush green vegetation and cascading waterfalls. We started slowly and gradually picked up speed. As we dropped, the trees and plants grew taller and birds began to sing. My senses were beginning to regain a sense of their fuller life. It was as if I was waking from the dead and every sensation was new. It then began to rain, and I delighted in the heightened aromas coming from the plants enveloping the road. We slept at Zhangmu and crossed into Nepal the next day.

We dropped another 800 metres to the border before starting the roller coaster ride in Nepal. The palette was full again: reds, greens, blues, yellows–in both flora and people. It was festival time in Nepal, so everyone was taking baths and doing laundry. The temperature was delightfully warm but not too hot. The breeze was a gentle kiss, and the slope allowed us to freewheel much of the way. Life was easy and fun as we zoomed through town after town. After a stop in Dulikhel, we pedaled to Kathmandu. Luckily, because of the festival, the roads were much less chaotic than usual, and everyone managed to evade being squashed by the erratically moving vehicles. Fifteen intense days of physical exertion delivered us back to Kathmandu battered but happy.

After a few days rest, Greg, my closest friend from the bike trip, and I headed out for a five-day trek in the Helumbu region. We had become buddies on the bike trip and decided to trek together. The Helumbu are the foothills of the Himalayas, and on a few occasions we were treated to amazing views of the snow-covered peaks. One night at sunset we climbed to the roof of our teahouse. Alpine glow blanketed the peaks, and I was able to pick out Everest on the horizon. At that moment, with no clue of how or when, I knew I would be back.

Chapter 3

DIVING BOARD

Faith is a process of leaping into the abyss not on the basis of any certainty about where we shall land, but rather on the belief that we shall land.
–Carter Hayward

APRIL 2006

As winter was giving way to spring, I was handed my lifelong dream on a platter, and after a long, hard week of pondering my options, I sent it back to the kitchen to be held under the warming light. As is often the case, I was fishing around the internet for interesting experiences. I typed in "Everest" and "fall" and Google delivered Wally Berg's website to me. Wally, a four-time Everest summiteer, was organizing a post-monsoon expedition to Everest called, "One Team, One Mountain." I dropped Wally an email to inquire about his expedition and received a warm reply with an invitation to call him. In a rare move, I picked up the phone and had a long conversation with Wally.

By the end of the conversation, Wally invited me to join the expedition. I don't remember driving home from the office because I was so pumped and excited. I could be on Everest in four short month's time–after a lifetime of dreaming. His expedition would be the only one on the mountain. He had two women on his team, and the team seemed strong and cohesive. How could I ask for more? After the initial elation, avalanches of doubt magnified by menstrual hormones pounded down on me, and I tried to swim to the surface to get some air.

In order to participate in Wally's expedition, I needed to raise $75,000 in one month, a near impossibility. While trying to raise the cash, I would also need to up the ante in my training, and prep my summer teaching. I knew deep inside me that I could pull it off, but some inner voice kept saying that this wasn't the right time. I needed more time to be ready for Everest. I saw climbing Everest as such a monumental task that I wanted and needed to spend enough time preparing.

I turned down Wally's invitation on the day I held my first Everest public fundraising event, "The Road to Everest." In one of the campus lecture theatres, I entertained a crowd of friends with pictures and stories from Denali and brought my Everest quest into public view. Tickets to the show, which nearly killed me to sell, generated the first $1,000 towards Everest. I stood in hockey locker rooms all the previous week holding tickets and trying to will myself to say, "I've got tickets here to my event in case any of you would like to purchase one." The chasm between the thought and the ability to speak the words was deeper than any crevasse I saw on Denali. Shyness won on Monday night. Tuesday I tried again, with shyness again threatening to engulf me in flames. But, I got strategic and enlisted the assistance of a friend to make the announcement. Wednesday I did not even try and Sunday I "forgot" to bring tickets to the game.

I came to understand that week that trying to realize my Everest dream would demand many new things of me. I have always been a quiet, shy person, so it was a big step to be so visible in the world. I knew that visibility was a necessary and vital part of the fundraising process but it stretched me almost to the point of breaking. I also swore to myself that week that I would not raise the money for Everest on the backs of my friends. Little did I know then, however, that the majority of the financial support for the expedition would come from my grassroots community.

Prior to meeting Wally on the internet, my plan had been to climb Cho Oyu during the fall of 2006 as a test to see if I truly wanted to climb Everest. Cho Oyu is the sixth highest peak in the world and is often considered a prerequisite for climbing Everest. Surfing around that day had changed everything. Wally had presented some compelling arguments for why I was ready to climb Everest, and he went so far as to suggest that Cho Oyu was "beneath" me. Considering the possibility of joining Wally's Everest expedition with the necessary fundraising that entailed, I found my focus and desire for Cho Oyu beginning to wane. I have never been particularly skilled at following more than one passion at a time, so I found it challenging to be preparing for two 8,000-metre peaks at the same time.

When I face a big decision, I often feel like I'm in the middle of a snow globe, a swirling snowstorm of options and considerations, and I can feel lost and overwhelmed. Fortunately, I have learned to be patient and wait because I know eventually the blizzard in my mind will calm and the way forward will become clear. I cannot force it, will it, or cajole it. I can only seek information, intuition, and others' perspectives. And wait. Then, at some point, the weather in the snow globe finally settles and I'm ready to actualize a decision. So, after Wally's invitation set off the internal blizzard, I was no longer climbing Cho Oyu; instead, I committed to climbing Everest in the spring of 2007.

By 9:00 a.m. the next day, I already noticed a change in me. With the pledge to climb Everest firmly in place, I began to push myself in new ways.

I picked up the phone, which for many is easy, but for me can be a mountain-sized challenge. I called a local business person I had met the previous weekend and asked him if we could get together to talk about potential partnerships. By noon I sent the climbing fee for a Mount Elbrus expedition. By evening I was telling the enthusiastic crowd at the "Becoming an Outdoor Woman" workshop, that I was climbing Mount Everest in ten months' time. I brought my "TA's Road to Everest" t-shirts to sell, and suddenly folks were buying them up in droves.

At these workshops, it's a tradition that the instructors gather for wine and tarot readings after the evening program is through. We were using a Russian gypsy deck—interesting considering I had just decided to go to Russia to climb Europe's highest peak. I asked the question, "How should I fundraise for my climb of Everest?" The cards were amazing and suggested success through exertion, remaining myself, and going out into the world. Card after card seemed to support how things were unfolding. We kept humming the theme of "The Twilight Zone."

I spent the spring and summer training hard for Elbrus. I put in long hours running, riding my bike, lifting weights in the gym, and hiking up Signal Hill with a twenty-five kilogram pack. I wanted to be ready for any challenge or obstacle Elbrus might put in my way. A month before the climb, I suffered a leg injury after running the Tely Ten Road Race and wondered if I would be able to heal in time for the climb. Shanna, the athletic therapist at Memorial University worked hard to help me heal. I went to acupuncture, massage, and physical therapy–wanting to support my body in every way possible. It wasn't until our first acclimatization hike in Russia that I knew I had healed enough to ascend.

Chapter 4

ELBRUS ENTRADA

The harder I work the more I live.
–George Bernard Shaw

AUGUST 2006

The last time I was in Russia, I was playing hockey. That was back in 1993 when I was in graduate school in Minnesota. I traveled to Saratov, Russia, to play in the Valerie Kharlamov Memorial Hockey Tournament in the first year that women were invited to play. Our opening game was against the "Witches of the Urals." We were glad to get out of the match with a tie, as several of their players were professional bandy players. Bandy is played on a soccer-sized ice sheet, with eleven players holding field hockey-like sticks, chasing a ball while on skates; it's often called "Winter Soccer." It was no wonder that witches could skate us into the ground. During the entire tournament, we were swarmed with fans and the games were televised. I returned to North America with a taste of professional hockey life and a silver medal.

This time I exchanged my hockey stick for an ice axe to pursue the summit of Mount Elbrus instead of hat tricks. At 5,633 metres high, Elbrus is an extinct volcano. It's the highest peak in Europe and one of the "Seven Summits." The Seven Summits are the highest peaks on each of the continents: Denali, Elbrus, Aconagua, Everest, Kilimanjaro, Vinson, and Carstenz Pyramid. Along with the massive goal of climbing Everest, I also set a goal of scaling all of the Seven Summits.

Elbrus dominates the western Caucasus Mountains like a two-headed giant. Elbrus is blanketed by an immense permanent snowcap that covers 145 square kilometres, and in some places is 400 metres thick. Long ago, the mountain was known as Strobilus, meaning pinecone in Latin, and reflecting the shape of the mountain's twin summits. It seemed fitting that the second of my Seven Summits would have two peaks.

We had a long wait in the departure lounge in the St. Petersburg airport. After a busy morning getting out of the hotel and transferring to the air terminal, my mind began to wander. I had watched the sunrise that morning being pleased that the same light would come early on summit day. Since arriving in Russia, our schedule had been full with sightseeing and meeting our teammates for the climb. Highlights were climbing the Bell Tower at St. Peter's Cathedral, a boat trip along the canals of the Venice of the North, and seeing where Pavlov worked and where the periodic table of the elements was invented. Seeing paintings by Rembrandt, Leonardo DaVinci, and a sculpture by Michelangelo stirred emotions deep within me.

There were thirteen in the group and I was the only woman. At the introductory dinner, our guide, Phil Erschler, paved my way into the group by highlighting my success on Denali using the Muldrow Glacier route. He didn't let my humility get in the way of promoting my competence as a mountaineer early in the group process. It was a brilliant guiding move that I deeply appreciated.

There was a nervous tension in the boarding area because the airline on which we were flying had had a plane crash the previous week. The plane was old and dilapidated. Everyone exchanged wide-eyed looks. Shortly after take-off, the plane started to buck and kick in some turbulence. More eyes darted around the cabin: many passengers gripped their armrests with tense, pale fingers. I looked through a rain-peppered window and spotted an enormous thunderhead. "Shit," I thought. "Lightning brought down the plane last week. I don't want to die in this remote corner of Russia." I held my breath and prayed to the universe for protection while trying to control the fear rising in my body. After a long hour of rodeo flight, we landed roughly in Mineralnye Vody. Every passenger cheered.

We collected the bags and stepped out into a dry desert heat. Sand flew across the parking lot assisted by a gusty wind. We crossed the concrete path to waiting vans and loaded a mountain of gear into them. I took a perch on the luggage so I could stretch out and sleep during the three-hour ride to Terksol. As conversation in my van was lulled into silence by the hypnotic road, I thought about the three climbers who had died on Elbrus the previous month. It's always sobering to hear of such accidents, especially just before I'm heading to the same mountain. In the week before I went to Denali, three climbers had to be rescued off Mount Logan, Canada's highest peak, and it really shook me up. Their accident gave my training a new urgency and focus.

Learning of the deaths on Elbrus, despite not knowing the circumstances, had the same effect. I made a commitment to be mindful every step of the way, to train both my body and mind, to listen to my intuition, to practise impeccable risk and hazard management, and to commit to both the summit and a safe return. It can take more courage to turn one's back to the summit than to press on, and I visualized such a decision in my mind over and over again as I trained. I've got a date with my best friend and some rocking chairs when I'm age eighty, and I'm doing everything I can to keep that rendezvous.

We arrived in the dark after being crammed into vans for the long ride to Terskol. We had a small hotel all to ourselves. Phil was kind enough to room with one of the clients so I could have a room to myself. I dropped into a deep sleep. The next morning dawned bright and I looked out my window at tall pines. After breakfast we headed out on our first acclimatization hike. Finally, after months of preparation, the expedition was underway. I was nervous about how my leg might do. We climbed from the valley at 2,200 metres up to an observatory at 3,300 metres and I was pain free. "Thank goodness," I thought, "I might actually get to climb this thing." We got our first view of Elbrus's twin peaks. As usual, the summit seemed so far away and impossible to reach. I reminded myself not to get caught up in how far away it was, and that all mountains are climbed step by step.

The valley's beauty invited feelings of awe. The lower arms of the mountains were ringed in a mossy green that gave way to a cliff-draped shoulder in a pale glacier scarf. The mountaintops were rugged, jagged, and caused everyone pause. The sky was radiant blue and the sun beat down upon us as it always does at altitude. It was good to get out and stretch my legs and lungs. I was pleased with how both felt.

The next day we hiked up to a nearby glacier to do some crampon training. I had more weight on my back as I carried up my big plastic boots, ice axe, and crampons. I felt stronger with a day of acclimatization in my possession. The glacier was dry with no snow so we didn't have to rope up. We practised many aspects of ten and twelve crampon technique and learned lots of French terminology from Phil. The sun was shining again and we saw Elbrus from a different angle. The summit was covered in a blanket of clouds, and I said a silent prayer for good weather. The best news from the second day was that my leg did well. I felt some pain at one point but then it eased off. I began to feel some hope that I had healed enough to climb. The acclimatization hikes and training brought the team together well. We ranged in age from thirty-six to seventy-six. Talk began to focus on the realities of a twelve-hour summit day that awaited us.

We were up early the next morning to put the final items into our packs, don climbing clothes, and head to the tram. One look at the tram had us all worried. Nervous energy abounded once again and lame attempts at humour tried to take the edge off. Twenty other people jammed into the tramcar with the team. We needed to be careful that we didn't spear anyone with our crampons and ice axes. The car whooshed out of the station and quickly gained height over the steep hillside. It creaked and groaned and complained about every metre gained. My heart rate jumped to match the rhythmic pace of the mechanical cacophony emanating from the tram. I wondered, "How quickly will I die if this car plunges from the overhead cable?"

To temper my rising terror, I distracted myself by thinking of home and the weeks leading up to being in this high perch, fearing for my life once again. I spent much of that final week before leaving feeling a sweet poignancy. The internal twinges of "I might not come back, this might be the last time I see this person, and wow, where I live is so beautiful," magnified many of my feelings during that time. I appreciated such reminders of my impermanence and felt them deeply.

I thought back to packing for the climb. I always vacillate during the gear selection process because I get stuck in a mindset of, "If I can only chose the right combination of things, everything will be okay. I won't be cold, hungry, wet." I constantly have to remind myself that most choices will get the job done, and that I will likely have moments where I suffer even with the best gear. Luckily, I relax once the decisions are made and the trip is underway.

One of my favourite outdoor jobs, and one with a steep learning curve, was when I worked with youth at risk. The program was based on primitive living, and so we slept in two wool blankets, carried our simple belongings in a rain poncho, started our cooking fires with a bow and drill, and all of our food for a week fit in a one-gallon Ziploc bag. Life was reduced to walking, talking, cooking, and sleeping. I remember, before I worked my first course, being scared that I would be cold, uncomfortable, and hungry the whole time. I left that summer with a desire to take much less into the wilderness with me because I had tasted the freedom of few belongings.

As if packing wasn't enough, I undertook a room renovation in the last two weeks before leaving for Elbrus. I painted and installed a new floor. Friends couldn't believe I was doing something so tasking before leaving. As the tram jerked upward, I realized that the renovation helped me deal with pre-climb jitters. Having a project to throw myself into kept the rising anxiety from overwhelming me. I finished the room just hours before boarding the plane.

After surviving the tram, we walked a short distance to an even more rundown single chairlift. I maneuvered myself into place to await the next chair, and Phil thrust my big pack into my lap the moment I sat down on the narrow seat. I chuckled at the long line of my teammates rising up the hill in front of me, each bearing his pack on his lap. I tried to find a more comfortable perch but quickly realized how easy it would be to fall, so I sat quietly waiting for the dismount station. We shouldered our packs and began the climb to our hut. The hut, located at 4,000 metres, was great. It had a dining area and two communal bunk rooms that slept eight apiece. This was our home for the next five days. We marveled at the luxury of staying in a mountain hut instead of tents.

The next day we gained 500 metres during another acclimatization climb. We were ready to try for the summit the following night. Seven hours into our first attempt, the summit seemed like a sure thing. We were climbing well and reached the saddle between the two peaks in good time. We were warm enough and the dawning light had finally broken through the thick, dark clouds. We had only 150 metres of climbing left when the wind accelerated to 100 kilometres per hour. The storm threatened to knock us off our feet and the visibility dropped to five metres. The weather made continuing foolhardy and near impossible. We turned our backs on the summit and consoled our disappointment during the three-hour descent to the hut.

Twelve hours earlier, the clock struck 12:34 and Phil said, "Let's go climb Elbrus." We rolled out of bed, choked down instant oatmeal and cups of warm tea. Out in the darkness we clambered to put crampons onto our boots. The path, barely lit by the single beam of my headlamp, revealed itself in step by step increments. *Crunch, step, crunch, step*, were the only sounds entering my ears. The mountain didn't seem so steep in the dark.

Step. Breathe. Step. Breathe. Step. Breathe. Step. Breathe. "The path is the goal. Don't think of the twelve hours of climbing ahead of you," I reminded myself. There was nothing to see but the pairs of boots ahead of me, nothing to see but black. About the time we needed light for our bodies and spirits, day broke with a golden light peering out from behind swiftly moving clouds. Now I could see the remaining steep pitch leading to the saddle. We took a break to drink and eat. The moment I stopped moving, the wind robbed heat from my body and I danced from leg to leg to stave off the cold.

Starting out on the steep incline, my mind begged for diversion. I thought back to the last month of training before Elbrus. I remembered sitting in my favourite chair with ice draped over various parts of my lower anatomy. It had been a tough training week. I fought fatigue and malaise the entire week and had to drag myself through runs and workouts. Severe knee pain showed up on two training hikes with my big pack. I wondered if my body was falling apart from the intense schedule I was keeping. The deep fatigue was draining my motivation and making everything seem like work. I kept pushing hard because I thought it was good practise to "work through fatigue" because that skill is required on big mountains. I have to dig deep and push on and up even when my body or mind wants to quit. I knew that my mind often wants to quit long before my body.

As we traversed the slope my mind played with ideas of light. I imagined I was climbing to the Great Eastern Sun, which in my Buddhist lineage is one of the symbols for enlightenment. The young light of day also spun thoughts of my Quaker times where I was taught to "Look for that of God in each person–to look for the Light within each." When someone was struggling, we would "Hold her or him in the Light." As I was held in the fresh golden rays, I also thought of how each day brings the opportunity to create, initiate, or commit.

Climbing into the new day reminded me that every moment is fresh. Each moment is all that there is, and if I can notice that, my surroundings and my mind become much more spacious. There is much uncertainty in our lives, but we can pretty much count on the sun rising in the east and setting in the west. The light that the sun sends changes in each moment. It also shifts over the course of the day, the season, and the year. Thick clouds or fog or night can hide it, but it is there even when I cannot see it.

The slope got steep enough to demand my full attention. I stepped in rhythm with my breath, slowly gaining altitude as the sun's light climbed over the ridge. The wind gained strength as we lost it. We climbed higher. The wind continued to rise. We reached the saddle between the two peaks and the visibility dropped to ten metres. The wind began to knock us around, sometimes even picking us up from our feet. When the winds reached 100 kilometres per hour, we knew our summit attempt was over. We needed to turn back. The weather had spoken and we had to listen. We turned our backs to the summit, turned our faces into the stiff wind, and beat our way back down over the next hours. Disappointed. Sad. Proud. I nurtured hope for another try.

Back at the hut, the mood of the group was very subdued. We had breakfast and Phil outlined the options. There was time in the schedule for a second attempt if the group wanted one. I was thrilled. Some folks instantly said they didn't want to try again. Other teammates said they needed to think about it. I kept my intentions to myself because I, most often, wait to see if something is possible before sharing my thoughts publicly. We all needed rest so folks headed into the bunks for a nap.

When the group next gathered, most had decided that they were done. They wanted to go down the mountain without trying again. I tried to lobby my closest teammates to give it another go. I began to lose hope. I didn't think Phil would remain with me on the mountain if everyone else descended. I went outside with my digital voice recorder and shared my feelings with it. Away from the group, my voice broke and tears flowed steadily down my face. I was so disappointed, both by being turned back by weather so close to the summit and by the unlikelihood of getting a second try. I couldn't imagine asking Phil to try again if I was the only climber left. I went back into the hut chastising myself for lacking assertiveness.

As I entered the hut, Phil began to make a plan for the next day's descent without asking me if I wanted to climb again. I stayed silent bearing my disappointment alone. A few hours later, Jeff awoke and joined the group. He had not been well, but was now feeling like he was over the worst of it. He told Phil that he wanted to give the summit a second attempt. At that point, I found my voice and echoed Jeff's sentiment. Phil said, "No problem. Let's make it happen." I was thrilled to be given a second chance and realized that I was more disappointed about not trying again than I was about not making the summit earlier that day.

After the rest of the group left to descend the mountain, Phil, Jeff, and I spent the day hibernating in the hut trying to gather strength and resolve in an ever-deteriorating weather situation. We watched the barometer drop through the day, the wind pick up, and snow begin to fall. We tried to stay positive that the weather would give us the break we would need. We had an early dinner and then tried to sleep before our first weather check at 11:30 p.m. We discovered that while the clouds had started to break, the wind was still high. We pushed our start back to 2:00 a.m. About 1:30 a.m., the sky was clear but winds were still howling. We decided to give it a shot, hoping the winds would ease as we got higher.

We dressed, forced down some chow, and headed out into the black night once again. The temperature was brisk and the wind unrelenting. With each step upward, we silently hoped the wind would drop. The wind thrashed us with snow pellets and each step up was a hard-fought victory. Looking up the slope brought a cutting face-load of snow. Three hours later, we huddled together with our packs blocking the wind, and with an even deeper disappointment stinging our hearts and minds, we made the hard decision to descend once more. We got back to the hut around 7:00 a.m. deeply saddened that the weather had again shut us down. We warmed up with hot drinks and breakfast, packed our bags, and descended to the decrepit tram.

Terskol welcomed us with hot showers and delicious food. Another storm ravaged the mountain that night and it seemed that no one would gain the summit. We explored the valley the next day and packed for the return trip home. After a wonderful celebration dinner in our hotel, we went to bed early because we had to start driving back to Mineralnye Vody in the early hours of the morning.

The moon beamed down a bright illumination onto the freshly fallen snow that blanketed the sleeping peaks surrounding us. There was not a hair of wind moving. The night was still and crisp. Elbrus would give up its summit today and we were driving away. Twenty-six duffels were piled in the van, sleepy people packed in beside, and Phil and I made eye contact–acknowledging that mountaineering is a sport of luck.

When I give motivational speeches, I show a slide that says, "The summit is when 10,000 hours of training meet hours of luck." During the climb of Elbrus, we experienced no luck with the weather. There was summit-friendly weather during our acclimatization period and as we drove out of town, but the time it mattered most to us, when we were standing 150 metres below the summit, luck was not with us.

"Abandon all hope of fruition" is one of my favourite Buddhist slogans. I reminded myself of it both times I set out for the summit of Mount Elbrus. It was a hard adage to actualize given that I had been training hard for six months, with the aim of standing atop Europe's highest peak. We had climbed over 2,500 metres in the two attempts and had not brought the expedition to fruition. In the traditional sense of mountaineering, we failed since we had not stood on the crown of Elbrus. For me, however, I measure success in mountaineering in multiple ways. Long after the despondent feelings passed, I remembered the golden dawn on the high flanks of Elbrus after hours of climbing through the night, the small acts of kindness and care in the harsh mountain environment, and the privilege of climbing with Phil Ershler, our guide, and one of the world's best mountaineers.

In Moscow, given the high price of hotel rooms, I had to have a room-mate. With a twinkle in his eye that I didn't quite understand, Phil paired Bill and I in a room. Bill had climbed all over the world with Phil. He knew of my interest in tackling Mount Everest and he pushed me to talk to Phil about it. Again, I was hesitant to give voice to that intention, but I kept watch for an opening. Part of the reason I had chosen International Mountain Guides to climb Elbrus with was that they were my number one contender for an Everest outfitter.

After a grand dinner, I headed to bed. The next morning, Bill told me that Phil had been trying to facilitate Bill and I getting together. I chuckled at the thought. When I went down to the dining room, my teammates seemed to be staring at me with funny looks. I walked up to Phil, put my hands on his shoulders, and said playfully, "Keep to matchmaking me with mountains." He got all tongue-tied and I went off to find my breakfast.

After a brief tour in Moscow, we spent hours waiting in the Moscow airport for our flight to Germany. I got brave and told Phil I wanted to chat with him about Everest. We found a time in the hotel later that night and I asked him, given what he had seen on Elbrus, if he thought I was ready for Everest. "Yes," he said, and then outlined his thinking that led to that conclusion. My extensive outdoor resume, especially my climb on Denali, had put me in good position to consider Everest. Back in my room, after our conversation, I found it hard to settle down enough to sleep.

"Phil thinks I'm ready, Phil thinks I'm ready," kept coming into my mind over and over again. Before eventually dropping off to sleep, I swirled with thinking that my dream might actually be possible. My mind took up where it left off the next morning, and during the long flights home, all I could think about was climbing Mount Everest.

Okay. I will admit it. I tried to take a donut to the summit of Elbrus and failed miserably. It wasn't just any donut. It was a Tim Hortons' Vanilla Dip. Some people question my fondness for this colourful, sprinkle-covered, childish donut, but I answer them by explaining that eating a Vanilla Dip is a religious experience for me. First off, I must always have a Vanilla Dip with a cup of tea. Balance. It's about balance. Yin. Yang. Sweet. Bitter. I can't have one without the other. Then, there are the multicoloured sprinkles on top. Colour cacophony. Crunch. Playful. Combined with soft, fluffy fresh-fried dough. Balance. Yin. Yang. My teeth pass by the crunchy sprinkles into the soft rush of sweet icing. I wash it down with a bitter swig of tea. In a matter of milliseconds, a universe of sensations combined with a rush of insulin and serotonin. With a bite, I connect with my inner child and the whole world looks brighter. Who could ask for anything more?

Early in my preparations for Denali, I adopted the Vanilla Dip as the official reward for training. At some point each week, I allowed myself to indulge in a Vanilla Dip as a special celebratory moment or when I need a sugar-sponsored boost. Once during a long, hard training week, I walked to a nearby Tim's and the woman behind the counter said cheerfully, "A tea and a Vanilla Dip." I was surprised because she had my order exactly right and I had only eaten there a few times before. I looked at her and said, "How did you know?" She said, "I remembered you because not many adults order Vanilla Dips." That's me, always at the edge of any continuum.

After two years, my relationship with the Vanilla Dip was stronger than most marriages. "How can I go to Russia without one?" I asked myself. I decided to take a Vanilla Dip to the highest point on each continent, and thought I should start with Elbrus. I polled my cyber support community for potential names for my sweet traveling companion. People rose to the occasion and submitted many names. I chose Velma because it means "protector." When going into high altitude mountain environments, one needs all the protection one can get. With that name in mind, I journeyed to Tim Hortons, selected the About To Be Famous Vanilla Dip, and took it home. It was hard not to eat it. I left it out to dry and shellacked it. Bad idea. Sprinkles and shellac don't get along very well.

I headed off to adopt another Vanilla Dip and set it out to dry. A few days later, I packaged it in a lovely round Ziploc container and put it into my luggage for the long voyage to Russia. Velma was a little nervous since she didn't like flying and hadn't managed to secure a Russian visa, but she made it through to Terskol. There, I unpacked all my gear and started sorting things into stay-low and go-high piles.

That was the moment when great sadness struck. When I opened the container to say hello to Velma, an amorphous mess of decomposing sprinkles and general stickiness greeted me. It seems that containing Velma was not a good idea, and she was in no state to try to summit Elbrus. At 2,500 metres in the lovely pastoral village of Terskol, her bid for the Seven Summits was truly over before it began. I fed her to a scraggly stray. It wasn't the ending to the story that either she or I had imagined.

When I returned to St. John's, many folks wanted to celebrate my safe return from the mountain by presenting me with my favourite treat. I had to eat a month's quotient of Vanilla Dips in that first week to both console my grief over Velma's demise and try to placate the donut goddess so she wouldn't curse my next expedition. By this point, I was so well known at the campus Tim's outlet that I could walk up and order, "A large tea with milk and a religious experience," and they knew exactly what I wanted. Sometimes I feel I need to justify my addiction to Vanilla Dips. In a fit of rationalization one day, I made a connection between prayer flags and Vanilla Dips.

I was talking on the phone in my office. My office is draped with a colorful array of Tibetan prayer flags and on my door is a picture of a Vanilla Dip. I was chatting away and suddenly it hit me that the colours of sprinkles on a Vanilla Dip are very similar to those on the prayer flags. Given that colourful crossover, a Vanilla Dip could then be reframed as an edible prayer flag whose prayers are not released by the wind but by eating them. Voila! Suddenly I was not eating Vanilla Dips for my own benefit, I was eating them on behalf of all sentient beings.

Not many people bought that argument but it made them smile. When I started to seek sponsorship for my Everest expedition, many people assumed Tim Hortons couldn't turn down such an aficionado of its donuts, and, in fact, would clamber to be involved. In reality, in months of trying to seek financial support, almost all corporate doors remained shut.

Chapter 5

NURTURING THE DREAM

Our life is composed greatly from dreams, from the unconscious, and they must be brought into connection with action. They must be woven together.
–Anais Nin

OCTOBER 2006

After Elbrus, I returned to training with a new focus, since the challenges of climbing Aconcagua and Everest loomed just three and six months later. As I designed the next phases of workouts that would culminate with the trek into base camp, I tried to incorporate the lessons learned from the summer about training intensity and overtraining. I lifted weights in the gym three times a week, attended yoga and Pilates classes, used running, step aerobics, and biking for aerobic conditioning, and hockey was gearing up once again.

For the past six months I had been saying, "I will climb Mount Everest if the fundraising comes together." Canvassing businesses since February had produced only one-sixth of the budget. On good days, I saw my fundraising efforts as preparing the ground for planting, tilling the soil, folding in compost, planting seeds, watering and weeding with hopes of a bountiful harvest. On the harder days, I wondered if the "garden" would be hit by desperate drought and the seeds would fail to germinate. At those times, I worried I might lose heart, so I continuously reminded myself to hold the view of Everest's summit while taking the steps that would get me there.

In presentations, I was struggling more and more with not being able to say I was definitely going to climb the mountain. I felt like a fake and my sense of integrity was floundering. Soon after returning from Elbrus, I met a friend for coffee and talked through my disappointment in fundraising progress. She said, "If you are not willing to pay for your climb, how can you expect anyone else to?" Her words struck me like an avalanche.

Soon after, I made a leap of faith, gaining an intimate understanding of why such moments are so named. Jumping into the abyss requires a decent helping of faith, a solid serving of courage, and, perhaps, a dash of wild abandon. I had been perched on the edge of a metaphoric diving board for half a year, knowing it would come to this: the big leap. This leap required me to step up to the brink, stare fear profoundly in the face, accept that I didn't know where the bulk of the money for the expedition would come from, take a deep breath, and hit the send button to transfer the deposit for the Everest climb to the outfitter.

With the non-refundable fee paid, I removed all of my escape routes. My words changed in that instant from "If I climb Everest" to "When I climb Everest," and my efforts towards fundraising redoubled. I now had an expedition team, an expedition date, and an expedition debt. I had to find $50,000 more or risk bankruptcy. The next morning, bathed in adrenaline from the big leap, I woke early and could not get back to sleep.

Before the sun rose, I sat at the computer improving my sponsorship package for the climb, and then designed a brochure about speaking to youth groups. After that, I baked a pumpkin pie, cooked a hearty pot of chili, and treated myself to an old favourite recipe of tofu. This was all before 10:00 a.m. It was one of those mornings when the universe conspired to remove all obstacles. Potentiality reigned. Later that day, my efforts were rewarded when I received my first sponsorship from a local company. I was elated and hoped several more would be on the way.

Early on Sunday morning, as I set out on my bike, I asked myself, "Where did my journey to Everest begin?" With each pedal cadence, I tried on an answer: "When as a one-year-old, chocolate plastered to my face, I learned to eat almost anything quickly? When, at three, I packed a butter and sugar sandwich and hit the road looking for adventure? When at twelve, I joined the Leaders in Training Program at the YWCA and began camping outdoors in the winter? When at sixteen, I learned to rock climb and got my first taste of mountain summits? When at thirty-seven, I saw Everest for the first time? When at forty, I climbed Denali and truly understood the responsibility I have in making my own dreams come true?"

My path to Everest probably began at all of those points. Life, indeed, is like a road with intersections and road signs serving as punctuation. Along the road to Everest there were lots of green lights, an occasional yield, and not so many parking lots. Having made the big leap into the abyss, I found a deep well of commitment, resolve, and fear within myself. I drew on each to find an extra edge in training, when imagining making a "cold call" to a potential sponsor, and when facing whatever the path asked of me.

Even at this stage I knew that the path would ask more of me than anything before, that I would have to dig deeper and wider, jump higher and farther, and do the things I thought I couldn't do to make Everest a reality, both in my preparations and during the climb. I named this edge my "Everest Edge," and I tried to play on it as much as I could. I needed to become familiar with it, touch it, feel it, run from it, run towards it, get used to its airy exposure, and practise staying there when what I wanted most was to get off and to stay off, when I most wanted to get on. This is the reality of edge play, a journey fraught with paradoxes and contradictions.

The edge was sharpest around fundraising. I polished my sponsorship package and then struggled to know what to do with it. I reached out to my support team asking them to introduce me to anyone they thought could be a potential sponsor. I felt confident that I could sell the expedition if I could ever find someone to sell it to. The prospect of setting up such appointments terrified me more than the thought of climbing Everest, so it was easy to put off making it happen.

As I began to speak at more and more schools, the mission of the expedition became clearer in my mind. I wanted the climb to serve others and to be "More than a Mountain." With this commitment in place, I renamed the expedition, "Everest-007," to focus attention on my intent to inspire youth. In jest, I imagined myself dressed as a mountaineering secret agent saying, "I'm Loeffler, TA Loeffler." I hoped to be a secret undercover agent who inspired kids without them realizing what I was doing. I chuckled inwardly at the double entendre of the name playing on James Bond and the year in which I was doing the climb.

I introduced the name when I paid my first visit to St. Francis of Assisi School in Outer Cove. During the previous week, the Grade Five classes had participated in a live internet expedition broadcast from a team on the highest peak in Ontario. I was able to answer lots of their questions about mountaineering. During the question period following my presentation, one boy asked me, "Will you come back to our school after you climb Everest?" I just about melted on the spot, and in that moment all of the trepidation of having paid the $17,000 expedition deposit from the credit line on my house also dissolved. I had the sense that if I kept reaching out, talking to kids and digging deep, something would come together on the fundraising side.

As the days darkened and warmth gave way to frost warnings and ochre-coloured hills, I continued to train hard and long. On the Friday before Thanksgiving I was climbing the stairs in the Education building over and over again. In some ways this seemed a bit pathetic and lonely. On the other hand, there wasn't much competition for the elevator. My friend Deb often told me that when she read my weekly updates, she either thought I was an inspiration or nuts. I was sure that once she read about my solitary ascent of the Education building, when everyone was long home in anticipation of turkey feasting, she would declare the latter once again, and I would have to agree with her this time.

I always preferred to get my training commitments done first thing in the morning, but sometimes life didn't allow that, so I had to suck it up and make it happen later in the day. It was always much more of a fight in the late afternoon than in the morning (and therefore much more of an accomplishment). It's funny how that works, because I know many folks who think exercising first thing in the morning is an excellent definition of torture.

During this phase in my training, I introduced "depletion days" where I would go out and perform intensive aerobic activity for hours on end, intentionally consuming less water and food than necessary. Sounds like fun, doesn't it? Actually, it was critical preparation for the summit push, where conditions or temperatures would likely prevent me from being able to eat and drink adequately. By practising hitting the wall and pushing through it, I gained familiarity with how my body reacted, what thoughts and feelings hunger and thirst brought up, and I trained my body to utilize different energy pathways.

The last "long day" of each training cycle became a depletion day. Talking on the phone one morning to a friend, I kept calling it a "deletion day." I was stuck with the image of the delete key on my computer keyboard–not the best image to be setting out with. I pondered during long sessions that such extended aerobic efforts often deleted my sense of self and I melded much more into the present moment. I became the grass swaying beside the road, the fiery palette of leaves lining the highway, or the waves crashing against the jagged cliffs.

Each training phase lasted four weeks followed by a rest week. Fatigue grew within me as the weeks of training built up. By the last days of a cycle, I felt like my body was encased in a flexible coating of concrete. I could move, but my limbs felt much heavier and slower than usual. It was a fatigue that crept in on silent kitty feet. Born of exertion that swelled both my muscles and soul with the warmth of accomplishment, it eased me into a sweet bath of endorphic lather and the sense that, ultimately, this weariness would bring the strength of body and mind that would serve me on the tallest mountain in the world.

A number of my supporters wrote and asked, "How many Vanilla Dips have you had this week?" I decided to nurture my inner quantitative researcher and conduct a small study entitled, "A Statistical Analysis of the Influences of Stress and Training Time, Duration, and Activity, on the Consumption of Multi-Coloured, Glucose-Encrusted Carbohydrates by Everest Bound-Mountaineers." I joked that I would be recruiting subjects for the study as soon as I received ethical approval for my research. In the meantime, I began to keep a running total of the number of Vanilla Dips I consumed during my training for the mountain. In hindsight, I can see a direct relationship between tough weeks and the number of Vanilla Dips ingested.

Because of training, I missed a turkey feast in Canada, but I had a second chance for Thanksgiving dinner in Leysin, Switzerland. Brenda and Jean-Marcel are lifelong friends. Brenda has known me since I was twelve when I was a Leader in Training at the Edmonton YWCA, and she once had the great fortune to see me profess my undying love to a Hobart dishwasher at summer camp. Jean-Marcel helped me survive first-year English at the University of Alberta and has been supporting my writing (and much more) since. Brenda, a teacher, lobbied her headmaster to bring me to Switzerland to speak to her school. Though I hadn't seen them in over three years, we dropped into the easy comfort of old friends and spent hours catching up.

Brenda organized a Thanksgiving dinner for all of the Canadians at the school. Given that I had missed out on the big bird meal in Canada, I was pleased to participate in the tradition of stuffing myself with the traditional fixings. I brought cranberry sauce from Canada to contribute to the feast. The dinner provided me with a fledgling connection with some of the students who I recruited to lead the dance moves to the Village People's "YMCA" that launched my presentation. Their gyrations quickly led to a Congo line and my presentation was off to a raucous start.

Though I didn't know it before my visit, Leysin has a long history of being the training ground for Himalayan climbers. I was actually the fourth Everest climber to speak at the Leysin American School in Switzerland–though the other three had managed to summit Everest before beginning their speaking careers. I spoke to the student body in two groups, and I was very pleased to receive the compliment that I was the first Everest presenter to deliver my message in a way that was accessible to students.

As I delivered motivational messages about tackling big dreams to the students assembled from over seventy countries, I too received a huge dose of inspiration. A few months earlier, Brenda touched me by informing me that she was dedicating her "cookie-fund" to my Everest climb. She baked batches filled with a delicious delight that only homemade can produce and the seventy boys in her care were eager for such treats. Joining her on cookie duty were three senior student salesmen who took Brenda's wares into the dorm and turned them into piles of Swiss francs. While I was visiting, I contributed to the effort by baking a few dozen cookies and brownies. The boys, through both charging a brisk tariff for the desired sweets and by soliciting pocket change on their dorm sales missions, transformed these into several hundred dollars of contributions to my Everest expedition. Each night I was moved close to tears as they turned over piles of coins that quickly added up to a substantial donation.

The Grade Ten English classes at the school were reading *Into Thin Air* by Jon Krakauer–perhaps one of the most famous Everest narratives. By coincidence, my trip corresponded with their study of the last chapters of the book, and I visited several classes answering questions such as "Are you scared?" "What things will you carry to the summit?" and "Do you think climbers belong on a sacred mountain?" I enjoyed stretching my mind around their questions, some of which I had not had the impetus to ponder before.

A cog railway can go seemingly impossible places. Brenda and Jean-Marcel took me on my first cog train ride from Aigle to Leysin, ascending some intensely steep angles I didn't know a train could manage. Between the two regular rails is a series of cogs that prevent the train from plummeting down the mountain against gravity. A reassuring "click, click, click" emanates from below the train as the cogs engage and disengage during the climb from the valley floor. I contemplated gravity and hoped to outwit it for a few weeks the next spring. Given some luck and my months of hard work, I aspired to push upward into mountain environs that few have had the privilege to tread. Like the cog railway, inspiration comes from, and leads to, the most unexpected and unlikely places. If I remained open, invitations and gifts surrounded me; I only needed to learn to accept them with grace and ease.

I returned to St. John's and jumped into the next phase of training. The pace of my life seemed extra crazy, but the contrast from the relaxation of Switzerland may have accentuated the difference. The changes in weather and daylight forced me to alter my training schedule, and I couldn't achieve as much in the pre-dawn hours. I really wondered about my sanity when I found myself trekking up the steepest hills of downtown St. John's at 6:30 on a Sunday morning, in the dark and in the pouring rain, wearing thirty kilograms on my back.

After a huge storm required them to rebuild their entire route through the Khumbu Icefall, Wally Berg's expedition managed to summit Mount Everest in late October. I was thrilled for them, wondered what it would have been like if I had joined his team, and thought it would be really nice to be done with the whole Everest thing right then. I emailed Wally my congratulations and read the account of the expedition over and over again before doing my long depletion day that week.

With my weekly Vanilla Dip count continuing to rise, a friend checked into Tim Hortons as a potential corporate sponsor. Their sponsorship agenda was full unfortunately, but they did mention it might be possible to provide me with all the Vanilla Dips I could eat (imagine that!) and all the coffee I wanted to carry up the mountain. While training, I daydreamed of drinking Tim's coffee on the summit, capturing the event on film, and then bringing back the image and selling it to them for many more dollars than sponsorship would have cost them on the front end.

Without any luck on the corporate front, I began a new phase of fundraising by ordering toques with the Everest-007 logo to sell. I had originally thought I would order baseball caps, but Judy suggested toques, as they would tie in better with a mountaineering expedition. She was right. By the time I left for the mountain, I had sold over 400 toques and could have sold more if I'd known we'd have such a long cold winter.

I had a hamster in graduate school. Her name was Gladys. She could bring smiles to the most staid members of the faculty. Gladys had a clear plastic ball in which she could freely roam the halls between classes. I revisited many of the fine moments I shared with Gladys as I climbed into the Hamster Ball during the Fog Devil's hockey game intermission. It was *I Love MUNDays* (spirit week) at the university, and I was asked to represent the faculty and staff in a hamster ball race.

Suited head to toe in hockey gear, I dove quickly into the clear, inflatable, human-devouring beach ball. The staff re-inflated it and zipped it shut. With the blower no longer causing hearing damage, I realized that I was indeed "The Boy in the Bubble," with my senses of sight and hearing muted by the vinyl casing. I was now officially a human hamster. Sealed sock-footed into the orb, I was granted membership as card-carrying affiliate of the "Officially Not-Claustrophobic Club." Using a combination of running and pushing, I rolled out onto the ice to the starting marker, lamenting the absence of my skates on my now chilled feet. I was racing the MUN Student Union president. I imagined the rink announcer creating high drama around the ensuing battle by pitting student against faculty, rodent against rodent.

Enclosed in my sensory-depriving sphere, it was difficult to tell that the epic marathon had begun. Noticing my delayed start, I called on Phidippides, the messenger who hurried to Athens to announce the Greek victory at Marathon in 490 BC, to invigorate my effort (though I dearly hoped to avoid his fate, as he died of exhaustion at the end of his heroic quest). Being a reasonably coordinated human hamster, I quickly caught up and broke into the lead until I was hip-checked by Scorch, the Fog Devil's mascot, and sent flying inside my ball. I met my opponent head-on behind the net and knocked her flying. Without further Scorch intervention, I sprinted to the finish.

Rolling off the ice, I was cheered by some girls on the concourse as I gave up hamster life and crawled out of the ball–a sweaty but exuberant adventurer. When I embarked on the road to Everest, I never imagined I would delay dinner at my boss's house in order to play hamster as publicity for the climb, but I was learning that I could never really predict where the road would lead.

The university held a lap-a-thon as a fundraiser for my expedition during the same week. One hundred and fifty five people showed up at the track to walk and run a total of 2,557 laps, the equivalent of fifty-eight Everests. Each residence hall collected loose change and then transformed it into some kind of mountain. The creativity was amazing, and I was touched by the efforts of the students. Actually, the entire event was very moving. Having a large group of folks turn out en masse to support the climb was a real boost.

NOVEMBER 2006

I bought some new bumper stickers for my car, The Oma-mobile. Given to me by my German grandmother, who we call Oma, the 1988 Chevy Corsica wears an ever-increasing coat of bumper stickers. Those who have little faith in my wondrous automobile chide that the bumper stickers are actually holding her together. I specifically got one to stick on near the lock on the driver's side. It was an Eleanor Roosevelt quote: "Do something every day that scares you." This was my new life mantra, and by placing it in a spot where I couldn't miss it, I made sure to push myself to live up to my intention. I knew climbing Everest would require that I manage, cope, feel, let go of, and be very comfortable with fear; thus I knew it was important to practise scaring myself.

Given my plans to climb Aconcagua over Christmas, I knew I would miss celebrating the holiday with my family. I tacked a few days onto a trip to Minneapolis, Minnesota for an experiential education conference to visit them. I showed pictures of my Elbrus climb and spent some time with Rayne and Xander, my niece and nephew. The visit was too short and I landed at the conference a bit out of sorts. The theme of the conference was "Out of the Box and Into the Circle." This theme aptly described my week there.

In my professional circles, I "came out" as an Everest climber. The conference's daily newspaper announced the expedition to all 850 attendees and I assumed a new level of visibility in the quest. Assuming a role of prominence and visibility was one of my major challenges and growth edges, as I would have preferred to keep a low profile prior to the climb. But Everest demanded much more of me.

My first presentation at the conference was to the Women's Professional Group. I shared some of the stories and images from my road to Everest, and the women were very moved and inspired by what they saw and heard–some being touched deeply by the idea of going after big dreams. I mentioned how I know that a dream is truly a dream: "I know something is truly a dream because when it first appears, it appears impossible." That perception of impossibility is a signal to me that I'm seeing a dream being born and I have to make a choice about whether or not to accept the invitation. One woman was so struck by the idea of "giving dreams" that she bought fifteen of my expedition toques and gave them as Christmas gifts. She added little notes about how she was giving both me and her gift recipients a dream.

I didn't train much during the trip away; I found it very hard to find the discipline. Instead, I used the week to rest and mentally prepare for the last four weeks of hard training before leaving for Aconcagua in December. Over the next month, I needed to manage the delicate balance of keeping the Everest mission moving forward, while getting mentally and physically prepared for the highest peak in South America.

After the conference, I settled back into home and training. During the first few days the huge number of tasks requiring my attention threatened to overwhelm me but I kept remembering that the only way to climb a mountain (and reduce a to-do list) was one step at a time. In continuing to take every moment and experience as part of my Everest path, I recognized that practise in dealing with overwhelm was a keystone in my training. Judy's dad arranged for us to meet the head of a local, large corporation. Eric greased the wheels, paved the way, and then turned the meeting over to me. I had prepared a customized audiovisual presentation, as I knew the images told my story in a powerful way.

After I finished showing him the pictures, the executive asked how far along I was in fundraising. When I said, "A third of the way there," he whistled and sighed.

"You've got a long road in front of you."

I answered, "I know that, but the climb is happening no matter what." His face betrayed his surprise and I said, "I mortgaged the house."

He got a bit misty eyed and said, "You embody commitment," a theme I had emphasized in the presentation. In the end, we had a grand chat and I hoped some sponsorship or speaking engagements would come of it. More importantly, I got my feet wet, faced some fear, and walked through some of my stuff about self-promotion. I appreciated Eric being there, as it felt like I had the benefit of training wheels during my first foray through the icefall of selling my expedition on the corporate stage.

Soon after that meeting, I found out that because of a miscommunication, I needed to submit another $10,000 to the expedition two months sooner than I thought. After a major inhale, I recognized it as another opportunity to cement my commitment to the process and thought, "Heck, what's a few more months of interest?" It gave me a greater drive to keep my fundraising program moving forward, while at the same time training intensely for both Everest and Aconcagua.

Fabien Basset, one of the exercise physiologists in the School of Human Kinetics and Recreation, allowed me to start using the "Go2Altitude" system in his lab. This very fancy machine allows athletes and aspiring mountaineers to train as if they are at altitude. I tried it out and spent ten minutes walking uphill at 4,000 metres as a test run. The system hypoxinates the air I breathe through a mask, and I could just watch my O2 saturation levels drop instantly. On Denali, we tracked our O2 saturation levels daily as we ascended the mountain. At its lowest, my O2 sat was 69 percent. Just to give that some perspective, if I walked into the ER here in St. John's at sea level with an O2 sat of 92 percent, they would likely put me in intensive care. During the first test run, we brought my O2 sat down to 71 percent and Fabien was amazed that I was feeling very little effect during the trial. Afterward, I did feel a bit off for a few hours: lightheaded, and a bit headachy—just like at altitude.

Through two local outfitters, I was able to order some of my clothing and equipment for my upcoming climbs at wholesale prices. One of the biggest decisions I faced was choosing my boots for Everest. After hours of research, I decided on the triple layered Olympus Mons boots, rated to temperatures of minus fifty-five, from La Sportiva. They were lightweight and I was eager to try them out on Aconcagua. I dealt with my ever-growing financial deficit by reminding myself that $69.00 a toe was a bargain for healthy, warm toes. Boots in hand, I once again visited St. Francis of Assisi School in Outer Cove. This time I spoke to the entire school. The school was kicking off its "Step by Step Healthy Living Challenge." The custodian painted a beautiful mountain on the gym wall. As the kids completed various physical activity challenges, a climber would move up the mountain. I loved seeing the eyes of the kindergarteners getting huge when I put my big Everest boots down beside them before starting my talk. After the event was over, I spent some time in both Grade Five classes. I could see that I was going to have a very special connection with those kids before the school year was out.

Along with St. Francis, I spoke to the Home Schoolers Support Group, an attentive audience of parents and kids aged three to fifty. The organizer baked cookies in the shape of my Everest-007 logo and sold them after my presentation as an expedition fundraiser. Judy had sponsored the printing of postcards to give away at such presentations. I tried them out with this group and the postcards were very well received. I saw them held proudly in small hands and I was even asked to sign my first autographs on them.

At the end of that week, I had been planning a big depletion day complete with drivers to drive me down Signal Hill after I climbed it over and over again, but I had to cancel it because I pulled my quadriceps tendon doing a squat during a morning workout. While enjoying a fabulous day in the gym and savouring strength increases on most lifts, I pushed the weight on the squat bar a tad bit too far and got some immediate feedback (though I did set a personal best). Ironically, I had said to myself that morning, "Be careful. You're extra tired and don't want an injury." The athletic therapist at work said it was a minor pull and wouldn't keep me out of action long.

I got off lucky: my mistake would not cost me Aconcagua. Instead, it was only a painful reminder to heed my inner voice. I had just finished reading Ed Viestur's book. He was the first American to climb all fourteen 8,000 metre peaks without using supplemental oxygen. He has a strong connection with his inner voice, and it kept him safe and healthy during thirty Himalayan climbs. His motto is, "The summit is optional, getting down is mandatory."

I spoke at the Boys and Girls Club in St. John's. It was an amazing experience. I could look out and see the ten-year-old girls "falling in love" with me. After the presentation, many of them came up to me and wanted to tell me their dreams, their plans, and check out all of the equipment. Usually I have to guard the sharps (ice axe and crampons) from the boys, but this time it was the girls.

One young woman from the group dropped me an email saying she realized that leaving her abusive boyfriend "was her Everest" and that she now wanted to turn her sights to a more positive Everest by setting the goal of running a half marathon by next July. I also heard from a woman who saw my presentation in Outer Cove. She thanked me for what I was doing by saying that she had recently been diagnosed with lung cancer and hadn't known how she was going to get through each day. Having seen my slideshow, she connected with my message of "One step at a time—just put one foot in front of the other," and was beginning to see her way through. I was deeply moved by these connections.

My focus on the big challenge of Aconcagua was becoming stronger each day. Because of the season, I spent much of the time training outside in the dark. It was a learning experience to notice the feelings of fear that arose in me because of the darkness. I was more thoughtful about choice of activities and routes. I worried for my safety and feared being attacked more than ever before. One morning I thought, "Wow, if I, as a very strong, very physically competent woman, can feel this much fear, how is it for other women?"

I knew that fear of attack is a huge constraint for women in terms of leisure and recreation, but now I really grappled with the enormous reality of this constraint. I pondered what, if anything, I could do to change it. With this, I set an intention for my Aconcagua climb. I wanted to have something to focus my mind and actions on while climbing or peddling or paddling–to have a cause to which I dedicate my efforts. For Aconcagua, I dedicated my efforts on the climb to the eradication of violence in all forms.

I tried, as I took each step up the mountain, to hold an image of a violence-free world in my mind. As a survivor of sexual assault, I know the enormous toil violence takes on both the individual and societal levels and I long for such suffering to come to an end. Although this was but a tiny offering, my hope was that by climbing with such mindfulness, I could make some small difference in the world.

As the time to climb Aconcagua neared, the pace of life continued to be just barely sustainable. I took the Everest-007 road show to Clarenville to talk to 500 kids in two schools, as well as the Rotary Club of Clarenville. It was a whirlwind day with three audiovisual set-ups and take-downs, four hours of driving and three hours of training. By the end of that very full day, it was still only Monday and I faced a week of similar days. My leg injury had the decency to heal quickly, so I was back to a careful but full training load. I continued to eke out strength gains in the gym and make progress with the hypoxic training. The Go2Altitude machine sucked the oxygen out of the air, so instead of 21 percent oxygen, I breathed 12 percent oxygen through my mask while walking uphill on the treadmill. My O2 saturation dropped a little less every day. Twelve percent oxygen is the equivalent of 4,500 metres above sea level. At the end of every session, I dialed down the oxygen a bit further to 9 percent in order to show my body "the summit" of Aconcagua. It was a real privilege to have such advanced gear to train with.

After surviving another big week of training, I attended a Buddhist program over the weekend. I spent hours and hours sitting in meditation. It's remarkable how "doing nothing" can be so exhausting. As was everything in those days, it was great training for Everest where patience and the ability to sit out cabin fever (a.k.a. tent fever) were critical. The theme of the Buddhist training was fearlessness, developing it and nurturing it, which went right along with my goal to do something every day that scared me. One of the messages of the weekend was, "You cannot know fearlessness until you've walked through fear." I came to understand that we don't lose our fear by running away from it, but instead by walking toward it. Pema Chodron, a well-known Western Buddhist nun, always tells stories of "running towards the biting dog." Trying to raise funds for Everest continued to feel like sprinting towards a Pit Bull.

Early on a Thursday morning, Judy and I began the drive out to Grand Falls-Windsor in central Newfoundland. Judy was originally from there and knew the highway intimately. Five hours later we arrived in time to grab a very quick bite and headed to Exploits Valley High School to do two back-to-back presentations. That night I spoke at a fundraising dinner for my expedition, and the next day I gave two presentations at Leo Burke Academy in Bishop's Falls before heading to Eastport to end the barnstorming tour at Holy Cross School. In all, I talked to over 1,000 young people and 100 adults. I loved every minute of it, though I was a crispy critter by Friday afternoon when we got back to St. John's. In thirty-six hours, we drove ten hours, presented six times, visited Tim Hortons six times, and slept very little.

After the big road trip, I took a night off and attended a performance of "Our Divas Do Christmas." It was fun to do something different. Listening to the Christmas music, it dawned on me that for all practical purposes, I was going to "miss" Christmas, and I got quite sad about it. After licking my wounds for a bit, I found a Santa hat and some candy canes to take along, Judy found me some battery-powered lights for the tent, and I planned to hang out socks on Christmas Eve to see if Santa delivered to high camp on Aconcagua.

I created an animated Christmas card to send out to my friends and family. I decorated a picture of Aconcagua with colourful balls and green garlands to look like a Christmas tree. I debuted the slide at a fundraising event and was delighted by the spirited giggles that went through the crowd when they "got it." We reached our fundraising goal for the event and started selling tickets for the next one. It was fun to reflect on how much the show and I had changed since the previous April when I launched the Road to Everest.

I now ended every presentation by asking the audience, "What is your Everest? What is a project or dream that would be like an Everest to you?" Peter, a seven-year-old son of a friend, attended the fundraiser. The next day it was his turn to give the news report to his class. He told them about my presentation and planned climb of Everest, and then asked his peers what their Everest was. Hearing the story as we dressed for a hockey game, I just about melted into a puddle on the locker room floor.

Three days before departure we had a snowstorm, and, in a heartbeat, I thought my Aconcagua climb might be gone. I went out to shovel snow and wrenched my back; it was the kind of pain that takes your breath away. I knew instantly that I had hurt myself, and I hobbled upstairs to stretch, get drugs, and sit on the heating pad. Fortunately, it was only a minor pull and with quick attention from the athletic therapist at work, I was back to almost full capacity in a few days. It was an intense lesson in impermanence and how quickly plans can change. I had planned to taper my training anyway, but the injury forced me to take a few days off earlier than I expected.

I used the extra time to pack and repack my duffle bags with the clothing and equipment that would keep me warm, dry, and safe on Aconcagua. My anxiety about an upcoming adventure always plays through when making gear choices, and this trip was no exception. I usually get into the pattern of thinking that if I can only pick the "right" gear, everything will be okay. Fortunately, I had enough experience to see the flaws in my thinking. I was not sure how the various pieces of the new clothing would work together, but that was part of the reason for the expedition. Aconcagua was a "shake-down" trip–providing the opportunity to test out my new clothing, gear, and training, as well as set a new personal altitude record.

I watched an Aconcagua DVD that a friend sent me. It gave a realistic picture of the climbing challenges. Much of the ascent would involve arduous climbing over rocky slopes, and there would be almost constant winds. I had been watching the weather reports for the mountain for the previous weeks, and it did seem like the winds had begun to drop. I hoped we would get the weather window we needed to summit. Aconcagua is famous for its sudden and vicious storms called "El Viento Blanco"–The White Wind. I began to pray that we would steer clear of such maelstroms. Little did I know just how much wind awaited me on the mountain.

Chapter 6

PATIENCE ON ACONCAGUA

All human wisdom is summed up in two words–wait and hope.
–Alexandre Dumas Père

DECEMBER 2006

After twenty-six hours of travel, I landed in Mendoza. The sun was still very high and the temperature a balmy twenty-five degrees at 8:00 p.m. It was great to leave St. John's winter temporarily behind. I actually slept pretty well on the eleven-hour overnight flight from Toronto to Santiago. It felt great to be back in Argentina, and I looked forward to meeting the rest of the expedition members the next evening. Over huge Argentine steaks, the team shared introductions and learned that our proposed climbing route had been closed by the National Park. To climb Aconcagua, the highest peak outside the Himalayas, we would use a hybrid route that combined the Vacas valley with the Guanacos route.

After dinner, I finished packing and noticed that I felt more relaxed than I had in days. My anxiety about a climb funnels around until I have made all my gear decisions; then it just melts away and I'm ready to go. I felt so bad for Liselle, my roommate, who was missing her bags and couldn't pack until the morning. I silently thanked the baggage goddess. The next morning we walked through Mendoza's famous square to the National Park office to secure our permits for the climb and to pick up last-minute items for some of the team.

We loaded the van and started the long drive to Penitentes, our jumping off spot for the climb. The road meandered through vineyard after vineyard before climbing through a slash between two mountains gaining altitude with every hairpin turn. The air was thin and brisk when we stepped out in front of the hotel. Dragging our duffels up three sets of stairs to our rooms left everyone gasping for breath. It was easy to tell that we had gained 2,000 metres that day. I started hydrating furiously to assist my body in acclimatizing to the new height and took a brief hike up a slope behind the hotel. The foothills, woven in shades of burgundy and sage, reminded me of many other desert mountains I had climbed. I felt excited to be out in arid landscape again.

We spent some time weighing and repacking bags for the mules to carry during the three-day trek to base camp. From climbers who had just descended, we learned that the weather had been very windy up high, and not many people had summitted yet this season. I gave a silent prayer that the weather would improve by the time we got there. Our team was truly international with folks from Canada, the United States, the United Kingdom, Chile, and South Africa, and we seemed to be coming together quite well.

With an early breakfast on board, we squeezed into two vans for the quick drive to the Vacas Valley trailhead. Already the temperature was hot, so Jason, the head guide, cautioned the team about sunburn and dehydration. After days of travel, I was glad to be hiking. The simple task of putting one foot in front of the other calmed the hormonal storm that my period had unleashed within me. The dry air and desert flora transported me back to the Grand Canyon of Arizona, and I spent some time revisiting past trips there. We trekked for six hours before reaching our camp for the night at 2,800 metres. Jason and Juan taught the group how to pitch the tents in a way that would help them withstand Aconcagua's fierce winds. I coached Sue and Liselle, my tentmates, in knots and camping skills.

A mountaineer from a neighbouring camp wandered over and struck up a conversation with the group. He had been up Aconcagua many times and wanted to share his expertise with us. At some point in the conversation, I learned he was Laurie Skreslet. I was the only person in our group who knew that he was the first Canadian to summit Mount Everest. I was thrilled, since I was meeting someone I had idolized since I was sixteen. Laurie summitted Everest the autumn after I spent the entire summer climbing in the Rocky Mountains of Alberta with my high school Outdoor Pursuits club. He and Sharon Wood, the first Canadian woman to summit Everest, were my heroes. As I listened to Laurie talk about Aconcagua, I began to get a sense of how cold it would be higher on the mountain. "I hope the guides can get everyone ready for such harsh conditions," I thought. I was one of the more experienced group members, and I hoped some folks were not in over their heads.

We climbed another 500 metres the next day. After arriving in camp, I chugged a quart of water because I could feel the hammer of altitude pounding on my head. There was great excitement because we had our first view of the mountain. Rising as a solitary, snow-covered sentinel from dusty, dry desert, Aconcagua dominated the head of the Vacas valley. We camped at Casa de la Pierdo, "House of Stone." In the alcoves of a huge rock, a stone shelter offered refuge to our mule drivers. They were hard at work preparing us an asado, a traditional Argentine barbecue. We enjoyed a hearty dinner and crawled into the tents for the night. No one slept much as the gusty wind caused the tents to shake and shudder violently.

A river crossing awaited us the next morning. Still in shadow, the frigid water seemed less than inviting, so I accepted a ride on a mule across the icy obstacle. We climbed up the steep side of a river gorge until we leveled out on the plateau that led to base camp. The wind was our constant companion, especially at lunch when it blew sand into every bite. We arrived in good time at the Plaza Argentina base camp, having climbed 900 metres from the valley below. The wind howled at about eighty kilometres per hour, so putting up the tents was a big challenge. Tents finally wrestled into place, we convened in the large dining tent provided by the base camp outfitter. Here we learned that several teams this season had been forced down from high camps when their tents blew away, and that only six out of 900 attempts thus far had resulted in summits. The group was somber at such news. "I sure hope the weather breaks and we get a chance," I thought. I had a boomer of an altitude headache that I hoped would soon pass.

With such a big altitude gain, we rested for acclimatization the next day. The following day, we were up early to do our first carry to Camp One. In a steep gully, we met some of the famous pentitentes: icy remains of snowfields sculpted into kneeling snow parishioners asking for their sins to be absolved. We'd all read about them, seen pictures, and from afar, thought of them as beautiful. Meeting pentitentes up close brought a different view: that of a slick, sharp, dangerous obstacle course that demanded agility, patience, and great effort to surmount, especially with thirty kilogram loads on our backs. After about six hours of climbing, we stopped below the last slope of pentitentes before Camp One. Caching our food and gear, we returned exhausted to base camp.

I'd spent much of the climb questioning everything, and my mind was filled with anxiety. Doubt was my shadow, even when the sun disappeared behind a cloud. Just at the point where I thought I might give it all up, we finally stopped to cache. A quick snack provided a burst of energy that I used to help collect rocks to hold the gear down. That extra exertion showed me I was not as done as I had thought. Even though I knew that the second carry is often easier, I dreaded the next climb back up to Camp One. When the going was really tough, I thought of all the kids I had spoken to, and the idea of disappointing them pushed me to take one step after another.

I once again recognized that altitude is the ultimate humbler. Because any rapid action resulted in severe panting and lightheadedness, and the prospect of speed was quickly forgotten. Slow. Steady. Rhythmic breathing.

One step, one breath. Even after being at altitude for days, slow was the only way. It's hard to imagine at sea level just how slowly we move at altitude. My memory is short; I had forgotten how hard each step is to take. Breathe. Take a step. Breathe again. Take another step. I imagine a slow moving sloth and try to move like him. Deliberate. Overcome the lack of oxygen with purposeful movement and conscious thought. It's like being drunk for weeks without the buzz, just the intense need for mindfulness and focus.

Back at base camp, I was trying to find the fine line between terror and preparedness. I'd spent much of the day imagining what it would be like on Everest. I tried over and over again to put Everest aside and just be in the moment on Aconcagua. It didn't help that Randy, one of my teammates, outed me as an Everest climber. He had googled all of us and discovered my "dirty little secret." I hadn't wanted this group to judge me through the lens of "She's going to climb Everest," so I'd kept my plans to myself. I was afraid it would put too much pressure on me if everyone knew. It was a funny mind game I was playing, but in many ways, it was also a relief to have everyone know.

We took another rest day to recover from the big carry, and then left base camp, hoping to not have to return. The streak of good weather had come to an end, and we arrived at Camp One in ninety kilometre winds and driving snow. Both of my tentmates were overwhelmed by the effort of reaching camp and dealing with the horrendous weather. I prompted them to action, and we pitched our tent, providing ourselves with a hospitable sanctuary. The tent often felt like a nylon cocoon. It was a safe place to rest, sleep, recharge, and escape the pounding of the elements. I marveled at how the thin walls offered such protection and respite, and I gave thanks for every gust they withstood. Inside its borders, the temperature would rise to bearable warmth, layers could be shed, and we had opportunity to think. The thin orange barrier held the line between life and death, comfort and pain, sleep and exhaustion.

I was grateful for my experience on Denali; it had prepared me well for Aconcagua. Instead of building snow walls around the tent as we had on the glacier, here we tucked in behind rock walls that other climbers had built over the decades. We added a few stones to the matrix and prayed that the tent would hold through the night. The next morning the sun returned but the wind remained. Sue made the hard decision to give up her climb and return to Mendoza. Her body just wasn't up for Aconcagua. Liselle and I were sad to see her go.

We took another acclimatization day and I explored around Camp One. Aconcagua, translated from Spanish, is "The Stone Sentinel." It is an apt name because it is a mountain of many rocks. Small rocks. Big rocks. Brown rocks. Dusty rocks. Talus. Scree. Gravel. I am surrounded by stone. My new Everest boots were beaten to a pulp by the rocks, but I was glad to get to know them. Erosion lives on Aconcagua. Both externally and within. New layers are constantly revealed. The mountain falls from the top. It's not the prettiest mountain, but, like wisdom-filled wrinkles in the face of a Navaho elder, there is rugged beauty in its failing flanks. There is solidity in standing when all else is falling.

It was solstice, the shortest day of the year in North America, and the longest day of the year at Aconcagua. Back in base camp, Jason had suggested that we carry as little as possible over the mountain. Listening closely to his advice, I sent my novel, playing cards, and journal back to Pentitentes on the mules. I kept only a pen, a few sheets of paper, and my Buddhist slogans. During that first rest day at Camp One, I instantly regretted my decision. I felt bored, claustrophobic, and wanting to be home. I had nothing to distract myself during the day or the night. I wasn't sleeping well, so I had spent much of the night consumed in feeling lonely, scared, wanting comfort, and missing the energetic, focused me.

The next day dispensed nicer weather so we carried a load to Camp Two. As we climbed, the views grew increasingly spectacular. I could tell I was further acclimatized because I climbed with a steady rhythm, and my mind was much easier to tame. We returned to Camp One feeling strong and optimistic. That night the wind picked up its fury once again and beat against the tent walls with relentless force. I hoped the guy lines would hold and that we would still have shelter by morning. At one point, I sat with my back to the wind, holding a corner of the tent down so it could not be torn from its moorings. Touching the thin wall stripped me of all warmth so I soon had to crawl back into my sleeping bag and hope that the tent could survive without my support. The morning brought light, but no relief from the wind. I sat bored once again, feeling a rising fear about Everest, with no entertainment to distract me from it. I hoped and prayed for a change in the weather. "Maybe the new moon will help," I wished. But when the next day spawned 120 kilometre per hour gusts again with an enormous lenticular cloud over the summit, I knew the new moon hadn't delivered.

What do you do when faced with a diminishing time schedule and 120 kilometre winds? We did as a Chinese proverb suggests: "We have little time so we must proceed very slowly." We had already been at Camp One much longer than we preferred. The weather forecast wasn't great, but every team except ours moved up. It was a delicate study in peer pressure and restraint that resulted in much prognosticating, gnashing, and impatience as we sat idly for our third day in a row. That night as the wind imitated runaway freight train after runaway freight train, our thoughts drifted to the higher camps, and we worried how the others were surviving such a vicious night.

The next day, as we sat once more, the mountain bled teams down its flanks. Battered climbers limped down from higher camps and fled the mountain in disgust after being hammered through the night by the unrelenting winds. We sat, unscathed, and able to climb higher the next day when the weather finally broke. Patience, in the impossible face of thinning time, was indeed a virtue.

Given the lost days to wind, we elected to try and bypass Camp Two. We broke camp and headed up the steep rocky slope towards the saddle. The climb was tough, given the forced inactivity of the past days. I reminded myself to just keep stepping when the inevitable doubt came calling again. A few hours into the ascent, I finally found my stride as we neared the windy divide. We stopped just below the high point to bundle up and have a quick snack. I sat on my pack enjoying the view, giving thanks that we were able to move again, and praying that the weather would hold. We needed five consecutive good days of weather to be able to summit, and the most we had had so far was two. Jason called the end of the break. We moved quickly towards our food cache, deciding to carry it all in one go to Camp Three.

Every cubic inch of my pack was filled, and there were a few items hanging off the back. The route climbed a gradual diagonal towards Camp Three on our original Guanacos route. The easier slope made such a difference. We stopped for a break about thirty minutes from camp. The temperature was dropping, so we kept it short. When we reached camp, we learned that two more members of the expedition had turned back because they were struggling with the altitude. We didn't get to say goodbye. They left some group gear at the break spot, so three of us volunteered to go back and get it while the others finished pitching the tents. This was the camp where other expeditions had lost tents to the wind. The protection walls were low or non-existent, so we did our best to build heavy-duty anchors for each guy line.

I returned to camp with my second load and dug candy canes out of my pack. It was Christmas Day at 5,800 metres, and I wanted to spread some seasonal cheer. I wished I had made the effort to carry up the battery powered Christmas lights from base camp, but since I didn't even bring a book, such excesses had to remain behind. The view from this camp stretched over several lower peaks to the horizon. I set a new altitude sleeping record and woke up feeling quite good the next day. We filled our packs and made a slow ascent to Camp Four. My doubting mind took the day off, allowing me to enjoy the continuous effort of gaining altitude. We cached our loads and quickly headed back down for another night of acclimatization at Camp Three.

I used one of my few pieces of paper to scrawl a journal entry about the hardships of living at extreme altitude. I knew this mountain was teaching me patience but also perseverance. "Hardship. That's life at altitude. Vision. Views from high places. Stark understanding. Rising above. Seeing nothing higher. Seeing in new ways. This is what makes the hardship both bearable and worth it. Seeing, and then coming down having seen. Pushing through. Giving up comfort. Working with my mind. Finding small pockets of fun and absurdity and laughter and connection. Seeing the morning light dance circles. Watching the evening sun drain from the hills. Sinking into a rich rhythm of physical exertion. Learning the lessons that come from days and days of outdoor living, the whispers of the stars, and the drone of the wind. All are my teachers and the mountains exact deep lessons."

The weather was holding, so the plan was to climb to Camp Four the next day and then try for the summit early the day after. When we moved to high camp, I really doubted whether I would even have a chance to try for the summit. After setting up camp and moving lots of rocks to make the tents super solid, a big jackhammer set up residence in my skull. A pounding headache battered my brain with the tenacity of a two-year-old wanting a treat in a grocery store line-up. Waves of anticipated disappointment washed over me and I slumped into the tent with my water bottle. I sucked back quart after quart of greasy snow-melted water and began to breathe deeply.

When venturing into environs where the body isn't designed to go, the mind needs to make up the difference. I must will myself to eat. I must will myself to drink. And drink. And drink. One litre for every 1,000 metres of elevation, so near the top I was drinking close to two gallons per day. What goes in must come out and both the altitude and the need to "dehydrate" always interrupted sleep. The twelve-hour nights became a series of catnaps interrupted by high-risk adventures with the pee bottle. Indeed, a urinary "incident" almost cost me my summit attempt by dampening my only set of long underwear. Luckily, I managed to get them dried in time. The smallest of details can stand in the way of the summit.

Water and air were the only hopes of mitigating the jagged throb that was now my existence. I lay in my sleeping bag drawing in deep breath after deep breath. I did the Buddhist practice of Tonglen, whereby I drew in my pain and the pain of all others with altitude headaches with every breath and then sent out relief with every exhalation. In. Out. Hope. In. Out. Can't ascend with a headache. Breathe. Drink. Hope. In. Out. In. Out. Hope. This is the only chance for the summit. In. Out. Can't ascend with a headache. Breathe. Drink. Hope. In. Out. Eventually it all worked and the headache eased, allowing me an attempt at the summit.

Jason shook the tent at 4:00 a.m. saying the climb was a go. I sprung up to begin dressing. It was extremely cold, so I planned to stay in the warmth of the tent as long as possible. Using hot water from my thermos, I made some instant oatmeal and choked down the pasty concoction between retches and gagging. This "wallpaper" paste is hard enough to eat at the best of times, but in the early morning at 6,000 metres, it was near impossible. I layered up and got the heat packs for my mitts going. I listened to how the rest of the group was progressing. When it seemed like they were close to ready, I popped out of the tent into the dark frigid night to put on my crampons. As the group headed out, I fell into line behind Jason. I prefer being near the front of the group.

With some exertion, I instantly felt warm and worried that I was over-dressed. I unzipped my parka and exposed my wrists. I felt panicky and claustrophobic. "Don't sweat," I told myself. "Sweat is evil." I took off my toque and began to cool down. The cloaking darkness always makes a slope seem less steep to me. I dropped into a stepping and breathing rhythm that matched Jason one for one. After two hours, the light crawled onto the horizon and we took our first break. Within minutes, I was chilled and eager to be moving again. I downed a GU, (a sickly sweet energy syrup in a squeezable tube), drank some water, applied sunscreen, and swung my arms to drive blood down into my hands. The slope steepened while the footing became more tenuous. One of my teammates decided to turn back shortly after the first break. An hour later, Jason asked another person to descend. Our numbers were dwindling and now Jason was the only guide with the group. "What if someone else has to turn?" I asked myself. "I hope it won't be me."

After four hours of climbing, we reached the "Windy Traverse." Since it was early morning, it was still in the cold shade and the wind funneled through at over eighty kilometres per hour. The traverse rose more gently than abruptly, but each step required more and more will to make.

I noticed that my pace was slowing and wondered, "Do I have it in me to summit today?" I thought about the possibility of stopping and turning around. I realized it would be okay to stop. Folks would understand. Then

I began to think once again of all of the children I'd talked to over the past year and remembered my friend Deb who got through the rigorous and dangerous journey of chemotherapy. I realized I couldn't stop just yet. Soon Jason called a break, and I hurried to get more calories into my system. My Powerbar was too cold to chew, so I took my last GU and washed it down with water. The cold stripped the heat from us rapidly, and we quickly began to move again. My steps become lighter and easier. I make a commitment to never make a "go down" decision without replenishing fuel first.

We stopped once more at the bottom of the Canaleta, the crux part of the route, for some food and water. Jason led us up the right side of the snow-covered gully. The footing was slippery and required exact concentration. Each step now demanded two deep breaths to have enough oxygen. A consistent rhythm escaped me, and I often leaned over my ice axe to catch my breath and slow my panting. As we neared the summit, Jason stepped aside and allowed me the privilege of leading the group to the top. I took the last step onto the broad summit plateau and saw there was no higher place to go. A smile graced my face. A big smile. I was amazed to be standing at the apex. We had gotten our Cinderella ending and our patience had been rewarded with a 360-degree view of the Andes.

After taking dozens of summit photos, we descended back to Camp Four dehydrated, hungry, and downright exhausted. I kept a good pace on the descent until about an hour before camp when I began to weave and wobble. I told myself to focus and get back to camp safe. After climbing for twelve hours, we hit camp. I began to toss back food and water to help my body recover from the Herculean effort and to prepare for the next day's descent to base camp. Liselle was very kind, and tended to me as I lay exhausted in the tent.

The next morning we plunged down 2,000 metres of scree slopes to be greeted by beer and pizza. We spent the afternoon in celebration, looking back towards the summit and asking, "Did we really stand up there yesterday?" At times, even now, I stop and ask the same question. After such a delicious lunch, I collapsed and spent the afternoon napping on a stack of plywood. Five days of intense physical effort with little sleep had finally caught up with me. The next day, we hiked for seven hours to the trailhead near Pentitentes. The hot showers and delightful meal fueled a grand celebration. Our team had been one of the luckier ones, having had four clients and three guides reach the summit. In fact, we had been the first to summit in over two weeks.

Reaching Mendoza the next day, the luxury of our hotel was a huge contrast to the hardship of high altitude living. It was New Year's Eve. We enjoyed some of Argentina's famous steaks and welcomed the New Year amid fireworks and revelers. Since I was flying out early the next morning, I returned to my room before the rest of the group. I reflected on the previous three weeks and wrote the following passage in my journal. "Alone. I alone must take the steps up the mountain. It is my will that makes the boots rise to meet the challenge. It is my heart that hangs in–in the face of huge avalanches of doubt–in the cold, dark sleepless hours of a high altitude night. But, it is the love and support, of those who have gathered me in their collective arms from afar, that keeps me stepping. I've come to count on the support circle that celebrates with me, commiserates with me, and fills me with inspiration when my tank is empty. Alone and together. That's what we are in this life, and on the mountains, and while at sea and at home. Both alone and together."

Forty-eight hours later, as I flew into St. John's, the pilot announced that we had just descended to 23,000 feet. I looked out the window amazed that I had stood at the same elevation just days before. Imagine. Standing where planes fly.

Chapter 7

PRIMING THE PUMP

Education is not a preparation for life; education is life itself.
–John Dewey

JANUARY 2007

I arrived back in St. John's after the dawn of the New Year. After the intense times on Aconcagua, I allowed myself to slide back into life slowly by taking the first week off from all physical activity. My homecoming was a roller coaster of both intense highs and lows. I had fun appearing on TV twice, giving radio interviews, and reading the media accounts of my Aconcagua climb. I was adjusting to my new life of "being famous," having people stop me on the street, in the bank, in the grocery store, and all over town to congratulate me on my latest summit. It was touching that folks were moved to do so, but I also found it a bit strange. I started training again on the first Monday because I felt rested enough to begin, feared losing too much ground, and I always like to begin things on Mondays.

A groin pull is every hockey player's nightmare. On my first stride of that Monday night's game, the dreaded sensation crept into my awareness. I skated gingerly for the rest of the game and went right home to my ice pack. I made the very mature (for me) decision to give up my Tuesday and Wednesday games to give the pull time to heal. I swathed it in arnica, took Epsom salts baths, and sent lots of healing energy towards it. I skated two Friday night games with it wrapped up tight and was thrilled that it did pretty well. Since I was leaving for Everest in nine short weeks, I was fortunate the injury was minor. I was aware that the time for healing was ever shortening, and I needed to be very careful not to get hurt. It was tempting to wrap myself up in bubble wrap, but I knew that hockey was an integral part of my training and, indeed, my life, so I played up until the night before I left for the mountain.

I continued to hear stories of people who were taking on new challenges, getting more active, and changing their lives because of what I was doing. I was moved every time. After I did the presentation at St. Francis of Assisi School in Outer Cove, they launched a physical activity program where the children contributed physical activity hours as a way of moving a climber up a mountain painted on their gym wall. The phone was ringing constantly, and I booked ten presentations in the first week I was back. I began to worry how I would manage training, teaching, fundraising, and presenting in the upcoming weeks.

Along with transitioning home, the first week back was filled with the intensity of loss. A student I was close to from the School of Human Kinetics and Recreation died. It was a tough week of grieving his passing and staring impermanence in the face. Michael loved to work out and frequently chatted with me in the Strength and Conditioning centre. He encouraged me to take supplements to help my body recover after big training sessions, and he was a big fan of my Everest climb. I knew when I faced tough times on Everest, the memory of his hard work and persistence as a student and athlete would spur me on.

Sundays were my long training days. My first Sunday back in training was a rare day when I didn't feel like training at all. It took a shoehorn to lever me out of my warm bed into the cold, dark morning. Trails were icy and the whole session was a mental struggle. At some point, the metaphor of a marathon came into my mind. I had been training for ten months, and due to the small taste of training freedom I enjoyed when I first returned from Argentina, I was now hitting "The Wall"–the part of the marathon where the body and/or mind doesn't want to go on. I thought it might be a time when I had to revert back to my system of rewards or treats to keep myself at it for the next two months. I knew that some days I would have to rely on pure will to keep focused and putting in the training hours. I reached out to my cyber community of support for encouragement to help propel me through the wall.

Walls are funny things. Sometimes they are solid, other times permeable, and sometimes they can be blown over by a wolf with big lungs. Walls separate, walls divide, walls stop progress, walls protect. Starting off the next training week, I continued to lag and struggle. Training felt hard and I didn't like being there. My first thought was to take a break and to stop the uncomfortable feelings by running from the gym. Buddhism had taught me, however, to stick with less comfy spots, so I just observed my mind, hung in, and made my way through my workouts.

I headed down to the lab for hypoxia training. I had a new training protocol that involved running intervals under hypoxic conditions, in essence a pretty tough workout. Given my mental state, I didn't know how the session was going to go. I got all hooked up to the machine and started the warm-up. When the beeper rang for the first interval, I began to run. Because of injuries, it was the first time I had run in months. And I ran and rested. Ran and rested. Ran and rested. Running at a decent speed on the treadmill while hypoxic took every ounce of focus I had. Very quickly I was sweating up a storm, dramatically out of breath, giddy from the exertion, and thrilled to be running again. I noticed that instead of running away from the wall, I was running through it.

Paradox had reared its confusing head once again. When everything in my being was screaming run away from exercise and towards inactivity, I found it was critical to actually run towards exertion. I did again as Pema Chodron suggested: "run towards the biting dog." Rather than training less hard that week, I trained significantly harder. I added five hours of training to my agenda and pushed myself through the wall. After my first step aerobics class in months (again because of injury), I knew the wall had dissipated and my training would become self-motivating once again.

By the end of the week, my body was filled with the lovely fatigue of seven days of intensive effort, and my mind was satisfied with its renewed commitment to the training process. It was a good thing, since the universe offered up another big challenge. Given the bitter cold weather, I spent much of the week camping out in my house without water. My pipes got hypothermia and refused to allow any icy cold water to flow through them. Fortunately, from years of outdoor living experience and a few other occasions of frozen pipes, I was well versed in strategies for getting along without running water.

Imagine my surprise when I came home from work on Friday and found my toilet just about to overflow. The pipes had thawed during the day, and the toilet ran thus sending a trickle of water down the sewer pipe that clogged the opening like a ripe case of arteriosclerosis. In a moment of unskilled problem solving, I flushed and sent the water cascading all over the bathroom and down into the utility room below. After I rescued my hockey gear from the flood, I threw down a gauntlet of towels to stem the flow. I deftly turned the water off at the toilet and began to reconstruct the events that led to the moment at hand.

I enlisted the help of my neighbor, Brian, to strategize the best course of action. We decided that I needed to thaw the sewer pipe, so I positioned a small heater to do the job and went to fix my supper. A few minutes later, I heard the toilet empty and I gave thanks for the easy fix. Then I heard gushing downstairs which is never a good sound. I rushed down to see the utility room now overflowing with a reeking, noxious brown liquid that won't be described further. I quickly ran to summon Brian, and we realized that there were two blockages, only one of which had thawed.

I turned to a miracle named the Shop Vac, removed its dry suck innards, and quickly tried to vacuum the unmentionable before it spread too far. Of course, I had to pause to think about why the universe appeared to have it in for me. There was no choice but to go with the flow as they say, and see if I could get enough cleaned up so as to not miss hockey. Having to clean up such a mess was a disaster, but missing hockey would be a travesty. Fortunately, the mighty Shop Vac came through, and I got the room to a state where I thought it could survive without my attention for a few hours.

I skipped the post-game refreshments to come home to my mini New Orleans. It was hard to progress in the cleanup since I still couldn't access the city's sewer systems. I recalled the actions of the plumber the last time he'd been here, and got brave and did what he did. I removed the trap and risked a greater short-term mess in order to achieve the long-term radical goal of water in, water out. After surviving the necessary brown geyser akin to Yellowstone's finest, I had access to the deep recesses of my plumbing and could send down boiling water to begin to dissolve the icy plaque that was stopping the flow. Four treatments later, very slow progress was achieved. It was now long after midnight and time for rest.

I woke up at four wondering about the state of the disaster zone and couldn't get back to sleep, so I went down to check. The hot water had finally done the trick, and I now had a functioning sewer again. With the modern conveniences of water and drain, I could begin the cleanup in earnest. I knew that so little sleep made a long training session out of the question, so I took the day off for rest and cleanup.

I've heard it said that, "It's a mark of leadership to adjust." That's what I learned from my frozen sewer ordeal: adjust, deal, don't cry over spilled milk or other unmentionable liquids, just set to, take it step by step, take frequent breaks, thank the chemical industry for Febreeze, change the plan, plan the change, and know that in the end, at some point humour will find a way to make any difficult situation bearable. Once again, I had no idea what awaited me on Everest, where I would need this same attitude to deal with a very messy problem.

I resumed my speaking program with an engagement at the Newfoundland School for the Deaf. I felt a deep connection with the audience and enjoyed the experience of speaking using an interpreter. I often use gestures while I speak, and I liked seeing how the interpreter signed things like puffer fish and crampon. It was great to be back speaking to young people and watching their reactions to my various stories.

I received a gift from my niece in the mail. Rayne was four and a budding artist. She painted me a picture of Mount Everest. She wanted to put me on the top, but there wasn't quite enough room so she painted a heart. Rayne's middle name is Amaris which means moon. Beside the summit in the sky, she painted the moon to watch over me. She put her handprint in the middle of the mountain so I would have a hand to hold when the mountain was steep. Despite the stormy cold weather, I melted on the spot. I displayed the painting prominently, and looking at it became a key part of my visualization practice.

Late in January, I welcomed my friend and Tibet bike trip companion, Greg, to St. John's. He came up from Los Angeles to film a documentary about my preparations for Everest. We had many fun times shooting scenes on top of Signal Hill in freezing drizzle, in a crowded Pilates class, and on a staircase in the Education building, among others. The process made me quite reflective about the whole Everest project and what it meant to me and to the community. I also shot a TV segment for a new local television show. Working with video rekindled my passion for filmmaking, but I knew I didn't have the time to indulge that during the last period of training for Everest.

I cut the ribbon to open the new Good Life Fitness Centre in the Village Mall. I hadn't realized ahead of time that I would be the only "celebrity" at that event. I was a bit startled when I looked around and realized I was it. They were very kind to donate a membership so I would have a state-of-the-art facility to train in over the next months. The Fog Devils hockey organization asked me to drop the puck at a game. They were having Ladies Night at the game and wanted a "cool lady" to drop the puck. My heart was beating wildly as I stepped out in front of the crowd. The game announcer told the crowd that the Newfoundland flag I was carrying was the same one that had been to the summit of Denali and Aconcagua and that I was hoping to take it to the summit of Everest. All Fog Devils stood up and were joined by many in the crowd. My eyes filled with tears by their gesture. I looked up and saw the Everest-007 logo on the scoreboard and knew the months of hard work were finally paying off.

After four weeks of tough training, the fatigue dog was catching up and about to bite. It was time for a rest week. I did a VO2 max test. Fabien, my colleague who did the test and who was helping me with the hypoxic training, declared that as a result of the test, "You are ready for the big peak." That had been my sense, but it was great to have it confirmed by objective numbers. My goal for the last phase of training was to maintain what I had, eke out a few more strength gains, and amass more cardio fitness before heading to Nepal for the ultimate VO2 max test.

A Grade Three class from central Newfoundland asked me to take Flat Stanley along to Mount Everest. Flat Stanley is a storybook character who had a bulletin board fall on him that left him flat enough to travel by envelope. Like me, Flat Stanley loves to travel and see the world. He brings backs stories and pictures from his adventures. The teacher had an artist do a rendition of a Newfoundland Flat Stanley, and he would travel attached to my expedition clothing. We received permission from the book publisher so that Flat Stanley could have his own website page during the expedition.

With a bit more time available to make decisions, I finally ordered the satellite phone and associated technology that would allow me to cybercast from the mountain. Learning about options and sorting through which ones made most sense in terms of features and cost had been a long haul. It was a substantial investment, but I knew it was critical to communicate with the youth of Newfoundland and Labrador throughout the expedition. Other pieces of gear ordered months before, like my down suit and minus-forty sleeping bag, began to arrive as well. My living room became the Everest staging area, with piles of equipment, clothing, and fundraising merchandise claiming all of the floor space.

FEBRUARY 2007

I was greeted by beautiful winter light as I emerged from my shelter. The night air had been brisk, but my new Everest sleeping bag was roomy, warm, and downright cozy. I had crawled into bed at about 8:30 p.m. and luxuriated in ten hours of "bag time," sleeping nearly all of it. I was with a group of students in the deep recesses of Pippy Park. They slept in quinzhees, a shelter made by piling snow and then hollowing out the middle. The weather was fantastic with the occasional fit of flurries to keep us on our toes. Being out in the snow, of course, turned my thoughts to Everest and the challenges of living in the snow for eight weeks. On the winter overnights before Denali, I was scared by the frosty temperatures and had wondered what it would be like to be out in the cold for five weeks. Now, several years later, that kind of cold didn't scare me anymore; it just reminded me to live carefully on the mountain.

The previous rest week, like so many other rest weeks, was overflowing with life challenges that filled my training space. It was almost as though the universe ramped up life during rest weeks just to keep me on my toes. Once again, the sewer was up to its old tricks by freezing and spewing nasty contents all over the back room. This go-round however, my wit was harder to find and the resulting emotions harder to tame. In the end, though, I was grateful for the life lessons of staying with frustration, working through hard spots, and eventually finding humour in the darkest and dirtiest moments. This time, I also learned how to ask for help. As I so profoundly thought, "When it's easy to ask for help, it's easy. When it's hard to ask for help, it's hard." I knew it would be critical to have the ability to ask for help on Everest.

Near the end of the rest week, my body caught up and resiliency began to rebuild in my body and soul. I woke before the alarm and I started to look forward to training again. That was always a sign I looked for to know if I had enough rest. After a year of fundraising, I was still $30,000 shy of my goal, so I put the Newfoundland Tricolour flag that I carried to the summit of Aconcagua for sale on eBay and tried to sell more tickets for my last fundraiser. Prepping my new presentation for this final event had me up past midnight several nights in a row. I enjoyed expressing my creativity and pushing the presentation software limits. I still secretly held out hope that a corporate sponsor would come through at the last moment. I continued to do three to four school presentations a week, and often added a community group. I felt like I was juggling many balls, and, as it seemed inevitable that some would fall, I hoped that I wouldn't drop too many. I vacillated between excitement and terror, energy and fatigue, focus and confusion, confidence and fear, trying in vain to find the middle way between all of them. I knew the next five weeks would be a roller coaster of emotions.

During my first week back at training, we were hammered by a huge storm that brought close to two feet of snow overnight. Shoveling was the order of the week, and everyone seemed to think it would be excellent training for me if I did all of their snow removal. I answered with, "Shoveling is the one thing I don't feel like I need to practise." I was thankful that the snow had the decency to hold off and let my fundraising event go forward. The new show was very well received and Greg's film was fabulous. I started using some of the new material I created in school presentations, and I loved watching the audience reactions to various part of the show. I was always relieved when they laughed at what I think are the funny parts. I ended each presentation with a question and answer session, and I was impressed at the astute questions the kids asked. I spoke to over 800 children that week bringing the total number of kids reached directly by Everest-007 to around 5,400. I didn't know that I would double that number in the upcoming four weeks.

The snowstorm facilitated some much needed time at home, and I did the first round of gear organization. The living room continued to be Everest central. I checked the equipment lists over and over again, waited for gear to arrive via post, and made shopping lists. With the luxury of time at home, life seemed to slow, and it began to look like I might be ready to go in a few weeks. There continued to be hundreds of details to take care of, hours of training to put in, leads to follow up, and website updates to do.

I attended a Buddhist training workshop. The timing was perfect. Mountains had been a critical part of my Buddhist path, and my Buddhist path had been a critical part of my mountaineering. It was often on the mountains that I got an embodied learning of the Buddhist dharma. I had been eager for the workshop and the teachings it would bring. The teacher spoke of daring, being a warrior, and about Right Effort. I had been thinking a lot about effort and exertion. I continued to feel that the training path had been long and I had become more aware of what I'd given up to follow the Everest path. On occasion, my mind drifted to post-Everest life, where time would likely be more spacious and I wouldn't have to ration my time so much. Right Effort has to do with discipline, gentleness, being present, and going with the flow. Not pushing through, but moving with grace and spontaneity. It was a timely teaching as I readied for departure.

My friend and marketing mentor, Wilma, wrote Tim Hortons suggesting they come on board as a sponsor. They wrote back saying that they get hundreds of such requests, but they would pass on the idea to their marketing folks. Most everyone said to me at some point that Tim's should be my sponsor, since I love Vanilla Dips so much. Along with the note saying "No," they did send $10 in Tim's Gift Certificates. I asked my cyber community to write Tim's and tell them about the wild Newfoundland woman who loves colourful sprinkled donuts. I hoped the mass appeal might loosen some sponsorship dollars, or at worst, finance my Vanilla Dip habit.

MARCH 2007

March certainly came in like a big African cat! On the first weekend of the month, I had students out in very stormy weather. I was proud of them as they put all of their semester's learning to the test while digging out their quinzhees in ferocious, blowing snow. As the afternoon wore on and the snow piled higher, I tramped from quinzhee to quinzhee checking in on each group. I pitched my tent thinking I would sleep there, but, given the big, gusty winds, I played hermit crab and dug out one of the leftover snow caves from the previous trip and crawled through the small hole to make my home for the night. I had brought my North Face Himalayan down suit to try out–the stormy conditions were a perfect trial. Looking slightly like a cross between Big Bird and the Michelin Man, I waddled warmly from group to group. I really felt like I was cheating but it was great to try it out. I made my first excretions through the "rainbow zipper," and it was amazing not to bare my bottom to the howling wind.

Those of us who braved the freezing drizzle to get the campfire going were treated to a spectacular view of a lunar eclipse. The clouds parted just in time for us to see the moon return after its time of darkness. The tiny sliver of light seemed to penetrate the sky landing right on the freshly fallen snow. It was a rare glimpse of skyward magic heightened by the contrast from the brutal weather earlier in the day. I was transported back to childhood and the infamous "snow suits" that all Canadian children of my generation went outside to play in. In my entire school career, we never had a snow day or even recess cancelled because of weather: we just bundled up and went outside in all conditions. I do remember once in Grade Five freezing my hands pretty good because I was punting a football at recess in minus twenty-degree temps. I preferred my bare hands to gloves because I could kick the ball farther. Perhaps, this explains a few things.

You have heard the cautionary phrase, "Be careful what you wish for–you might get it." I thought to myself, "High up on mountains, folks often sleep in their down suits, perhaps I should try sleeping in mine." About an hour after that thought, a student came by saying that she'd ended up with a scrap of a sleeping bag instead of one of the school's new winter bags. I paused and thought. I quickly realized that I needed to give her either my down suit or my sleeping bag. Since I was currently snug in my suit, she got the minus-forty summit series sleeping bag. I got my hood, my summit gloves, and my boots. She had a toasty night. I missed having covers.

I crawled into my quinzhee, pulled on my neck gaiter, positioned my hood, and put my backpack over my pad where my boots would lie. I had also taken my big Everest boots on the trip because I had to replace the pair I had climbed in on Aconcagua due to a bad zipper. They didn't have my exact size to send back, so I had to go up one size. It was funny to try to sleep with no covers, and in big boots and a fluffy hood. I curled up and was pretty warm through most of the night. Getting up in the morning was also simplified since there was no warm bag to have to get out of into the cold.

After the cold weekend, time seemed to speed up once again, and I worried that my to-do list was getting longer instead of shorter. I spent hours with my new personal digital assistant learning to post to my website. As with all technology, some parts of the learning curve were smooth and quick, others were laborious and frustrating. I wondered what I had undertaken in wanting to send dispatches from the mountain. I continued to speak to schools. I often used the metaphor that we all have an inner puffer fish that blows up inside us and pokes us until we pay attention to our dreams. At one elementary school during the question and answer period, a girl in Grade Five put up her hand and said incredulously, "So ALL of this was because of a puffer fish?"

When I asked the group, "What is your Everest?"

A young one in Kindergarten put up her hand and beamed, "My Everest is to be a butterfly."

I faced one last big week of speaking at schools, and I visited eight including a road trip to Placentia. It was also my last big week of training. Eighteen months of sustained preparation was rapidly coming to an end, which meant that I must be going to Everest! I actually had trouble saying that out loud or even to myself. Denial was easier. I managed my fear and anxiety by breaking it into phases. I could only think of it as trekking into base camp, then climbing Island Peak, then the first trip through the Ice Fall. Anything more than that brought avalanches of fear and doubt.

Zachary Davis, a student in the third grade class that sent me Flat Stanley, dropped by my office with his dad to meet me. He brought a tape recorder and conducted a most professional interview. He knew his class-mates had some questions, and so he wanted to bring the answers back. I gave him some prayer flags to take back to his school because they had a large Everest painted on the wall, and I thought the prayer flags might be the finishing touch. Mrs. Stoodley, the teacher, also came by the house to meet me. I loved hearing about how the school was embracing the climb. Like St. Francis of Assisi School, they would move Flat Stanley up the mountain as the children completed hours of physical activity. Her class held a candy sale to raise money for the expedition. She presented me with a cheque. We hugged and I promised I would bring Flat Stanley back to her school in June.

My last week in St. John's began and ended with send-offs. Several friends gathered one night to wish Flat Stanley and me well. It was precious to see everyone, and one of the highlights of the night for me was the Vanilla Dip Timbits. When I learned six months previously that Tim's could make them as a special order, I knew I wanted them at my send-off party. They were an absolute delight to ingest—mini-religious experiences in every sprin-kled, self-contained bite.

My last send-off was at MacDonald Drive Junior High School on the last day of their spirit week. I did my last presentation and the school cho-rus did a very moving version of "There Ain't No Mountain High Enough." The media was there in droves, and it was a terrific ending to the speaking program of the expedition. In all, I spoke to over 10,000 kids in the province in the previous ten months.

With the parties, packing, and goodbyes done, it was time to embark on the big adventure. As I finished packing, I realized that I couldn't find Flat Stanley. After ripping the house apart, I found him in the T-shirts pile. My two huge duffels weighed 30 kilos each. I had all the tech gear in my carry-on, and I hoped the big snowstorm predicted for the eastern seaboard would let me off the island. Little did Mr. Hamilton, my high school English teacher, know when he introduced me to rock climbing and mountaineering in 1982, that twenty-five years later, I would be heading for Mount Everest.

Chapter 8

TREKKING THROUGH
THE PAST TO BASE CAMP

We all have our time machines. Some take us back, they're called memo-
ries. Some take us forward, they're called dreams.
–Jeremy Irons

Two days after my send-off from St. John's, I arrived in Nepal to climb Mount Everest. After settling into my hotel room and taking a quick shower to wake up, I took my first foray into the luscious chaos of Kathmandu. Horns sound constantly because dogs, motorcycles, cars, trucks, and people share the same road in a tenuous harmony. I reminded myself to look the other way, since they drive on the left here. I wove up the sidewalk as if drunk, trying to remember which way I was supposed to pass other pedestrians. I was caught between my old and new worlds, not having fully left the old one, and not truly in the new one.

Slowed by thirty-six hours of travel and 8.45 hours of time zone change, I was still able to find my way to Thamel. Greeted by the aroma of incense and the familiar melody of "Om Mani Padme Om," I felt like I was home. But the thought that I wasn't in Nepal to trek, but to climb Mount Everest, was never far from my mind. I vacillated between facing reality and using denial for comfort; in the end I thought only of the first step, the trek into base camp.

Thamel is the tourist Mecca where I spent most of my time in Kathmandu during past visits. The narrow streets are lined with shop after shop and colours and sounds abound. The push of humanity through the streets is the lifeblood of the tourist existence here, and touts competed for my attention on every corner. Every few steps, I turned down offers for treks, clothes, shops, drugs, and rickshaw rides. I marveled at finding the rickshaw driver I rode with five years ago. I promised him another ride when I returned from Everest. In 2002, he let Liz drive his rickshaw and he rode in the back with me.

After lunch at Momotarou, my favourite sushi place in Thamel, I did some email to let folks know that I had arrived safely and found my way to Raj's office. We spent the afternoon catching up on news, and then I went to his home to share dinner with his family. The streets of Kathmandu are empty at night, evidence of the long difficulties with the Maoists. We finally found a cab to take me to my hotel. I wilted as the excitement of arriving drained and deep fatigue set in.

I slept deeply and awoke the next morning when the cacophony of bird songs entered my consciousness. As I had left winter in Canada, I hadn't heard a bird in months. It was still early, so I did something different for me: I watched TV before tackling my gear duffels. I wanted to remind myself of what was in each bag. After a few hours, I headed back over to Thamel and looked up an old breakfast haunt, The New Orleans Café. Greg had found this gem tucked away in a garden on a side street. I reveled in eating outside and read the English daily paper to catch up on Nepal news.

A bit later, I met Rupa, Raj's wife, and she took me over to Boudhanath Stupa, one of the holiest Buddhist sites in Nepal. The stupa is located in the heart of the Tibetan Buddhist community near an ancient trade route to Tibet. Merchants offered prayers here for many centuries. When Tibetan refugees flooded into Nepal in the 1950s, many decided to live around Boudhanath, so numerous monasteries, shops, and restaurants surround the stupa. A popular tourist site, the ancient stupa is said to entomb the relics of a guru venerable to both Buddhists and Hindus.

I first visited Boudhanath with Liz and Raj in 2002 on the day after Tibetan New Year. The stupa was adorned with thousands of prayer flags newly hung at the previous day's celebration. Something deep within me stirred that day, and I make at least one pilgrimage to Boudhanath each time I visit Kathmandu. Devotees circumambulate the stupa clockwise and many perform prostrations at its base. Rupa and I climbed high on the stupa and walked around our perch three times. I filled my mind with thoughts of Everest. I remembered that Jamling Tenzing Norgay sponsored the lighting of 50,000 butter lamps on Boudhanath before departing on his expedition to climb Everest during the fiftieth anniversary season of his father's climb. Tenzing Norgay and Sir Edmund Hilary were the first to climb Mount Everest in 1953.

Returning to ground level, I spun prayer wheels and asked for safe passage on the mountain. We made our way back to Thamel, and Raj took me to Chetripathi to buy prayer flags. There is a small stupa there with a surrounding Buddhist community and many wholesale prayer flag stores. As always, it was quite a negotiation. Raj helped me sort through all the sizes and materials. I knew I was jetlagged when I returned to the hotel and counted the number of strings I had purchased. I was aiming for fifty strings and managed to buy ninety. I noticed how differently I related to the Buddhist iconography in Nepal on this visit compared to previous ones.

As my knowledge and commitment to Buddhism grows, the ever-present imagery holds much deeper meaning.

Raj's brother, Krishna, helped me carry the prayer flags to my hotel. As I entered, I met Mark Tucker, the expedition leader, who said, "There's been a change of plans. Because of a potential strike on Thursday, we're heading into the mountains tomorrow."

I rushed out and called to Krishna, "I won't be able to meet you tomorrow. Please tell your brother I'll call when I am back from Everest."

Mark explained how to organize my duffels for the trek up. "One bag will go directly to base camp and the other you will have access to during the trek." I headed up to my room to get organized before the team dinner that night.

"Tomorrow! We're starting the trek tomorrow," I said excitedly to the chirping birds outside my window as I began to sort the clothing I needed for the trek. Fortunately, when I packed at home, I had already put all my high altitude gear in one bag. I recognized the familiar sense of anxiety that filled my belly at that moment. "Am I making the right choices? Can I do without that? How much snack food do I need?" My thoughts raced. "Stop, breathe, and relax," I lectured myself. "You have already trekked to Everest base camp, you know how to do this."

I thought back to the previous Everest climbing season when I had followed Paul and Fiona Adler's climb of Everest with great interest. Paul and Fiona were sending updates from the mountain to their website. It was the first time I followed an Everest climb on a daily basis, and I cheered loudly when Fiona summitted and cried with disappointment when Paul was stopped short by an oxygen problem. Paul decided to try to climb Everest again and had designed a website called "My Everest" to which he would post updates. Somehow, Paul and I hooked up over the internet and he invited me to post to the site as well. I had been planning to just phone in updates to my website but with Paul's coaching, I now had the ability to post text and pictures as well. With only a few more hours left in Kathmandu, I had to get the system working.

I headed up to the roof of the hotel to try again. I had the satellite phone, personal digital assistant (PDA), folding keyboard, and lots of cables to connect them. I had followed Paul's typed instructions to the letter the day before but hadn't gotten the system to connect. I hoped I would fare better today, since we were flying to Lukla the next day and I wouldn't be able to email Paul with my questions. I tried Paul's latest fix with no luck. I emailed him from the hotel computer and headed off to dinner with my team. "At least you have the ability to post audio updates," I reminded myself to console the disappointment.

Most of the team was assembled in the lobby when I arrived. It was a large group with summit climbers, Camp Three climbers, and base camp trekkers. Mark handed out a group list to help us see who was climbing what, and we met some of the guides and staff. Tentative conversations began on the bus ride to a nearby hotel where we dined in the courtyard beneath a blanket of stars. Kathmandu had rotating brown-outs, and because our portion of the city was dark, lit only by portable generators buzzing in the night like swarms of gasoline powered mosquitoes, we could see the stars easily. Nervous laughter filled the table as Mark described the next day's flight to Lukla.

"There will be an early team and an earlier team," he joked. The lucky folks on the first flight had to be up at 3:30 a.m. to be ready for the first flight of the day. I was thankful to be in the second group, since I still needed to give the technology one more try. I checked email again when I got back to the hotel, and Paul had given one more suggestion. I got out my headlamp and went up to the roof again feeling a tad bit like a spy or secret agent. Holding the phone to the sky, I finally heard the sound of the modem connecting, and I sent my first text-based update to the site. "Hallelujah," I exclaimed to the surrounding night and headed down to try and get some sleep.

Sleep, of course, was hard to come by. I tossed and turned while my mind filled with doubts and worries. I hoped that the anxiety that was fueling my restlessness would ease in the morning when we actually started trekking. At breakfast, I learned I was not alone. Most folks had had similar nights that were reflected in their drawn faces and heavy eyes. After tea and toast, we organized the duffels and headed for the airport. The domestic airport was bustling with people, gear, and cargo. We watched the Sherpa[1] staff negotiate the chaos with aplomb, as they had done this many times before. Their easy calm settled us all down. The word "sherpa" refers to both an ethnic group of people in Nepal and to the job of assisting climbing expeditions. Not all climbing sherpas are Sherpa, but most are.

The twin otter sat twelve on each side of a small aisle. With our daypacks on our laps, we joked about the plane having airbags. The flight attendant handed out balls of cotton for our ears and sweets to suck on. The plane was not pressurized. We rumbled down the runway and began the climb out of the Kathmandu valley. Clouds occluded the view of the snowy peaks to the left of the plane but we could see the green terraces of the

---

[1] When referring to Sherpa people or culture, I will capitalize the word. When referring to the job of sherpa, I will not capitalize the word.

foothills quite clearly. The drone of the engines crept beyond the makeshift earplugs and filled my head with a vibration that made it hard to hear myself think.

I could see the pilots through the opening to the cockpit. They were peering through the thickening cloud cover trying to get a glimpse of the valley that would lead to Lukla. My heart beat faster as we skimmed over a pass without much clearance. "Please don't let me die up here," I asked the universe. We circled around and then the pilots gunned the engine. They spotted the runway and wanted to get the plane down before the clouds closed the gap. The Lukla airport runs uphill at a steep grade to slow the planes down on landing. A cheer went up on the plane as the wheels touched down. "I'm not the only one who was scared," I thought.

We disembarked and walked a short distance to a teahouse where we met up with the earlier team. We had another round of breakfast and started trekking towards Phakding.

I had no inkling of the circumstances that would unfold to bring me back to this same teahouse two months later.

After months of planning and training, it was so good to start walking. The movement eased the fear and anxiety out of my system, as life became the simple task of putting one foot in front of the other. Out of Lukla, the trail dropped considerably and then followed the valley that the Dudh Kosi carved out. In Nepali, the word "Dudh" means milk, and the river runs silty white because of its glacial source under the snowy peaks of the Goyko region. Carving its way down this valley to the Ganges in India, the river has allowed people to inhabit this region for centuries.

I spent much of the day grappling with fear of failure and wanting to quit the expedition before it really began. So in Phakding, I spun my first prayer wheels of the trek asking for determination, courage, and confidence. Gentle rain began to fall, but then turned into heavy sheets as we arrived at our camping spot. Daphne, a new acquaintance from South Africa was my tentmate for the trek. She and I moved into our tent once our duffels arrived on the zopkios. A zopkio is a pack animal used at lower elevations in Nepal. They are bred by crossing a yak and a cow. Yaks cannot survive below 3,400 metres.

Daphne, who was trekking with the expedition to base camp, had not camped much so I shared some of my strategies with her. Because I didn't have a system yet and the tent had several leaks to avoid, everything felt chaotic since I changed my clothes and ran between the raindrops to the dining room that our staff had secured for our use.

The warm heat from the fire created a cozy atmosphere to type my first update, drink some tea, and eat some popcorn. Popcorn was a staple at tea time, and I began to look forward to the salty snack each day. Given the early start, I headed to bed shortly after dinner. In the tent, I reflected on the day and realized how comfortable I was in both living outdoors and in Nepal. I vowed to carry that ease into the next day and to reach out and start building connections with the expedition team.

The rain stopped overnight making packing much easier the next morning. After a few hours of walking, we stopped at the entrance to the Sagarmatha National Park to show our climbing and trekking permits. Sagarmatha is the Nepali name for Mount Everest, which is translated as "Head of the Sea." Nepali folklore describes that when the Himalayas emerged from the sea, Sagarmatha was the head, the first thing to appear, and, of course, it remains the highest point. At this stop, one of the trekkers realized that he was not physically able to handle the challenges of trekking at altitude, so he left the group to return to Lukla.

As I trekked, I remembered many more of the sights and sounds of the Khumbu valley. Passing teahouses where Liz and I shared a meal, or crossing suspension bridges over the Dudh Kosi, memories tugged at my heart repeatedly and I was transported back to 2002. I smiled each time I was greeted with "Namaste" (I greet that of god in you), and hearing it signaled that I was back in Nepal. I thought, "How lovely to be greeted in such a way so frequently. Perhaps the world would be different if we truly recognized that of god in each person." I repeatedly brought myself back to 2007 so I could drink in the colours, smells, and sensations of the trek. I couldn't go far without the aroma of dung or woodsmoke filling my nostrils.

After some boulder hopping, we had lunch at the base of the "Namche Hill," a 600-metre ascent that awaited the group. Nervous banter went back and forth during the meal, and many were anxious to start the big climb. Trains of zopkios carrying reams of gear to higher locales passed frequently. Humility was dished out at similar intervals when I noticed that porters wearing flip-flops using baskets to transport loads that weighed almost as much as I did, were outpacing me. Porters tend to carry the loads that are too big, too awkward, or too weird for zopkios. I saw fifteen-foot pieces of PVC pipe, corrugated tin roofing, plastic garden chairs, and one large television going up the trail on porters' backs. I noted in my journal that, "I passed the TV and the TV passed me and then I passed the TV and now the TV just passed me again."

As it turns out, the climb, like most anticipated challenges, was easier than I expected. I dropped into a groove and powered up the hill at the front of the group. Nearing the top, I felt like I had finally fully arrived in Nepal. The meditative hike, connecting breath and step, lulled the discursive thoughts that had been plaguing me. I arrived in the horseshoe-shaped village of Namche Bazaar full of excitement and a sense of wonder, and in time to organize gear and get things dry. I had a funny thought while I trekked: "Training for Everest was like prep school, and the trek in is like finishing school." Altitude does funny things to my thoughts.

Namche, located at 3,440 metres, is the main trading center for the Khumbu region, so there are many government officials, a police check post, an army barracks, shops, and a bank. The village has been considered the gateway to the high Himalayas since the first climbing expeditions. Our lodge was located at the very top of the hill, so we had one last climb to end the day. We were rewarded for our effort with a commanding view of Namche and the surrounding peaks.

A chorus of dogs competing for the loudest bark punctuated the night. Morning came bringing an enchanting light and lofty views of snow-covered peaks. After breakfast, most of us headed up to the Everest View Hotel to catch our first view of the mountain. The hike provided us with a chance to stretch our legs and breathe deeply while we introduced our bodies to the new altitude. The idea was to climb high and sleep low as a way to acclimatize. A person acquires functional acclimatization about one week after such an introduction, but complete acclimatization requires four to six weeks. Acclimatization cannot be rushed, only supported. The climb up from Namche was steep, and starting out from each break winded me. I reminded myself that this was normal at altitude, and to just keep stepping because my heart rate would stabilize once I found a rhythm. I felt stronger as the hike progressed.

As we rounded the corner above Sangboche, Everest came into view. Many in the group began to point and speak excitedly. I sank quietly into my thoughts wondering what awaited us when the climbing would finally begin. Using binoculars, we tried to identify landmarks on the peak. One thing that did not escape our notice was the huge plume coming off the mountain, indicating the presence of high winds on the summit. We hoped the plume would disappear during "summit week," six to eights weeks down the trail.

Flat Stanley was very excited to see the mountain so early in the trip, so I took his picture to post on my website. After a snack at the Everest View Hotel, we descended back to our camp for lunch and then ventured down to the village to do some email. That night several of us played a raucous game of rummy before turning in.

From our high perch above Namche, the blue, red, and green roofs of the village formed a vivid patchwork of colour reminiscent of a Sherpani's apron. Soon after breakfast, we headed down to town to explore the weekly market that draws folks from neighbouring villages and as far away as Tibet. The market was packed with people and goods: spices, recently slaughtered meat, packaged food products, and plastic Chinese shoes were piled high. We squeezed through the crowd and then explored Namche's cobbled streets.

While in town, I met my personal climbing sherpa, Mingma Ongel Sherpa. At first, I thought I registered a look of disappointment in his face. Was he dismayed that I was female or by my height or something else about me? Fortunately, I managed to drop the idea and remain open to building a strong climbing relationship with him. I had been impressed with his performance on summit day during the previous Everest season when he climbed with Fiona so I requested him specifically. Fiona had advised me that Mingma was quiet and less forthcoming than some of the other sherpas on the team.

Later that afternoon, we had our official meeting with the team of personal sherpas at camp. I took the lead in conversation with Mingma and learned he was going to take a course at the National Outdoor Leadership School (NOLS) during July. I told him that I instructed for NOLS. He seemed impressed. I asked Mingma about his village and family. He is from Phortse, a three-hour walk from Namche, and has a wife and two children. Many on the sherpa team were from Phortse since Ang Jangbu was also from there. As each sherpa introduced himself, we learned that the team had seventy-six collective Everest summits. Mingma had summitted four times!

In talking with Mingma, I learned that Sherpa children are often named for the day of the week on which they are born. Mingma was born on a Tuesday. If I were Sherpa, since I was born on a Thursday, my name would be Pemba. In Nepal, people's surnames represent their ethnic group. After about thirty minutes of conversation, I wished Mingma a good trek up to base camp, but the anxiety about meeting him was still present. To help calm my mind, I reminded myself to trust that Mingma and I would grow to become a good climbing team.

Our trek doctor, Luanne Freer, arrived in the late afternoon. After spending some time together, we sorted out that we had met before in 2002 at the Himalayan Rescue Association (HRA) clinic in Pheriche. She had diagnosed me with high altitude gastritis from drinking too much Nepali tea and prescribed some medication to ease the severe heartburn I was

Left: The team ascends a steep wall to regain Karsten's Ridge to complete a carry of supplies to Camp Five.

Photo credit: TA Loeffler

Centre: TA proudly flies the Newfoundland flag on the summit of Denali (Mount McKinley), North America's highest peak. (6194 metres)

Photo credit: TA Loeffler

Bottom: The summit ridge of Denali as seen on descent. The huge mountain in the background is Mount Foraker.

Photo credit: TA Loeffler

Photo credit: Greg Rainoff

TA at the summit of Gyatso La pass in Tibet (5250 metres). Having ridden 38 kilometres uphill on her bicycle, TA was dehydrated and impaired by the altitude. This is evidenced by her inability to hold the Newfoundland flag in its correct orientation. TA knew she "wasn't all there" so in the next photograph she reversed the flag to ensure she got it right in the end.

Photo credit: Greg Rainoff

The north face of Mount Everest as seen from the Rhonbuk Monestary in Tibet. After bicycling to the base camp on the north side of Everest, TA knew she wanted to undertake the challenge of climbing Mount Everest.

This is evidence of the incessant wind at Camp One on Aconcagua. Notice how the tent fly is smashed against the tent wall. TA's team was pinned at Camp One for days before the wind broke.

Right: TA posing with a fake apple on the summit of Aconcagua (6959 metres). She "borrowed" the apple from the office of AppleCore Interactive, her communications sponsor. TA took the apple on the climb and photographed its many adventures. *Photo credit: Jason Abbott*

Climbers struggle to make headway in big winds on Mount Elbrus, the highest peak in Europe. Snow picked up by the wind flies at the climbers' feet.

A climber makes his way through pentitentes, a snow formation unique to the Northern Andes, after making a carry to Camp One on Aconcagua, the highest peak in South America.

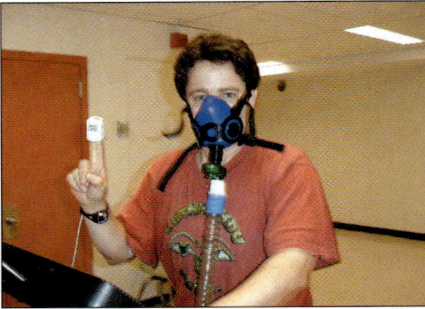

TA using the Go 2 Altitude system to train hypoxically before Aconcagua and Everest. Through the mask, TA breathes 12% oxygen which simulates 4500 metres in altitude promoting both acclimatization and greater fitness.

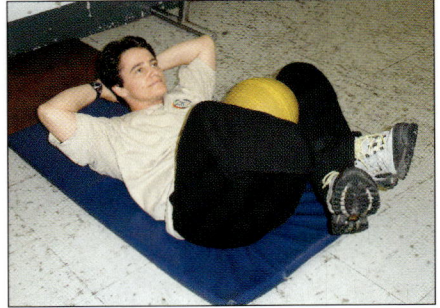

Core strength helps mountaineers carry heavy backpacks loaded with food or fuel. TA doing crunches to build her core.

TA working out in the Strength and Conditioning Centre at Memorial University of Newfoundland. Leg strength is very important to mountaineering. At her prime strength, TA could leg press 750 pounds.

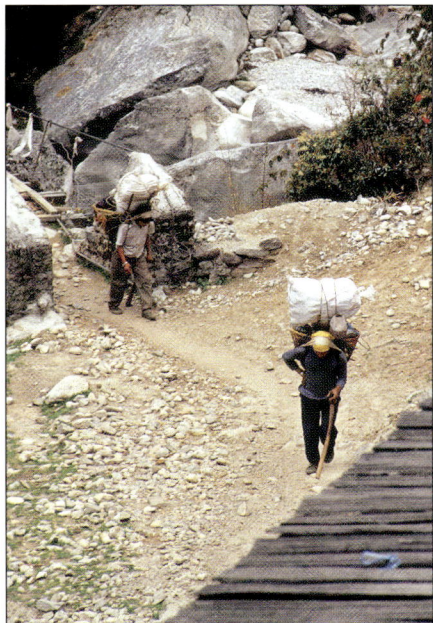

Photo credit: TA Loeffler

Porters carrying loads of supplies towards Everest base camp. Loads in their baskets can range from 20-40 kilograms.

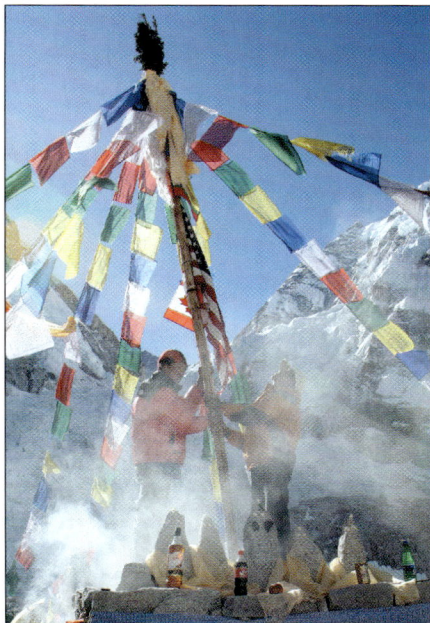

Photo credit: TA Loeffler

Sherpas raise the pole of prayer flags during the Puja ceremony at Everest basecamp. A Buddhist lama asked for the mountain's blessing before climbers began to ascend the Khumbu icefall.

Photo credit: TA Loeffler

TA's teammates, Al Handcock and Tim Warren, light butter lamps at the Deboche Nunnery to ask for protection while climbing Everest.

A zopkio pokes its head into the Tengboche Monastery. A zopkio is a beast of burden produced by crossing a cow and a yak. It is used at lower elevations where yaks cannot go.

The summit pyramid of Mount Everest (8850 metres) as seen from Kala Pattar, a trekking peak.

Most villages in the Khumbu region of Nepal have a monastery that sits high above the town. Here, the Namche Bizarre Monastery is festooned with prayer wheels that are spun as people walk by.

Left: Climbing sherpas celebrate during the Puja ceremony. Mingma Ongel Sherpa, TA's personal sherpa, is seen second from the right wearing an Everest-007 toque. The sherpas have tsampa, barley flour, on their faces for good luck and long life. *Photo credit: TA Loeffler*

Centre: Everest base camp is built right on the Khumbu Glacier resulting in "gravel-pit camping to the max." The ice, constantly in motion, pushes glacial moraine along its tops and sides resulting in an inhospitable living area. *Photo credit: TA Loeffler*

Bottom: Spindrift snow from a nearby avalanche coats climbers during a training session on the lower reaches of the Khumbu Icefall. *Photo credit: TA Loeffler*

TA descends one of the many ladders in the Khumbu Icefall. The ladders allow climbers to bridge crevasses and climb overhanging sections of the icefall with greater ease.

TA crosses a ladder over a deep crevasse in the Khumbu icefall, stops halfway, and snaps a picture of her boots and the ladder.

Mingma Ongel Sherpa climbs a ladder to nagivate a steeper section of the Khumbu Icefall.

Mingma Ongel Sherpa makes his way through two towering columns of ice at the base of the Khumbu Icefall.

Mingma Ongel Sherpa traverses "Ladder Three" in the Khumbu Icefall. The route and ladders through the icefall are maintained by a group of sherpas called "The Icefall Doctors."

Left: The tents of Camp One with Pumori on the left in the background. The large dome was our cook tent.

Photo credit: TA Loeffler

Centre: Two climbing teams meet at a ladder in the Western Cwm.

Photo credit: TA Loeffler

Bottom: The view from Camp One looking up the Western Cwm towards Camp Two and the Lhotse Face.

Photo credit: TA Loeffler

Photo credit: Judy Cumby

TA presenting her message of "Big Dreams, Big Goals" at Holy Trinity Elementary School in Torbay, Newfoundland and Labrador.

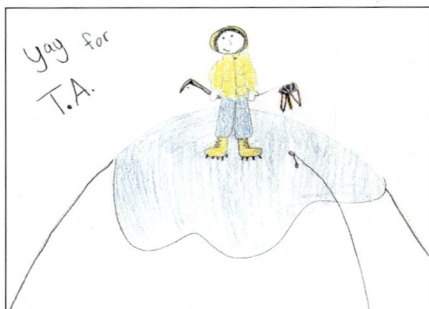

Photo credit: TA Loeffler

A drawing TA received from a student at Stella Maris Academy in Trepassey, Newfoundland and Labrador.

Photo credit: TA Loeffler

A note of encouragement from a student at Stella Maris Academy in Trepassey, Newfoundland and Labrador.

Flat Stanley being held on the summit of Mount Everest by Jean Ricard during an acclimatization climb to Pumuri Camp One.

Photo credit: TA Loeffler

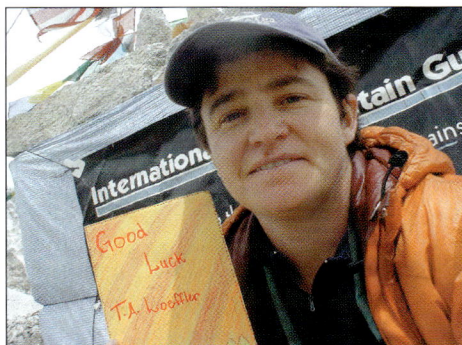

TA holding a good luck card she received at Everest base camp. The card traveled from Newfoundland via jumbo jet, then by Twin Otter, then by porter and finally by yak. TA called it yak mail!

Photo credit: TA Loeffler

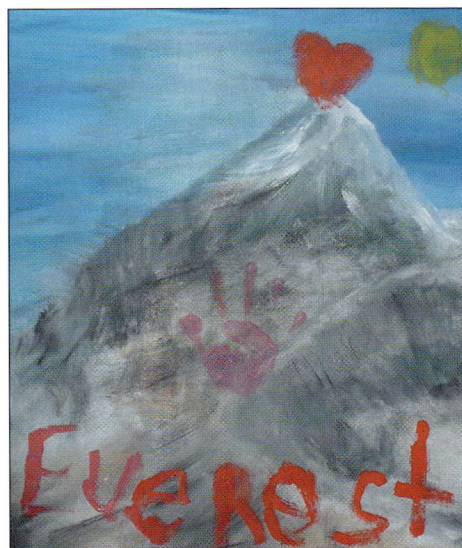

Photo credit: TA Loeffler

The picture of Mount Everest painted for TA by her niece Rayne, who was four and a half years old at the time.

Photo credit: TA Loeffler

The inukshuk that TA built to honour the memory of Michael Beecher Smith. The inukshuk was built on the shoulder of the Khumbu Glacier with a view of Everest's summit.

Two climbers offer scale to the massive ice seracs of the Khumbu Icefall.

TA showing the effects of having Giardia at Camp Two.

The shadow of Everest's summit pyramid after a long dark night of climbing.

The traverse to Everest's summit with terrifying drops to either side.

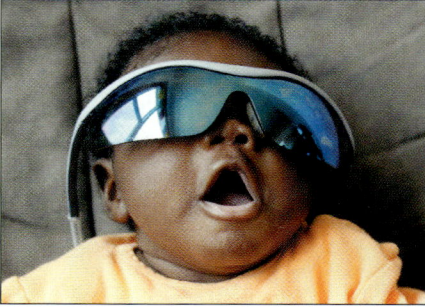

Takunda models TA's sunglasses.

A picture is worth a thousand words. TA waiting for her flight from Lukla to Kathmandu.

Flat Stanley nearing the summit of a scaled version of Mount Everest at Woodland Primary School in Grand Falls-Windsor, Newfoundland and Labrador. The children of this school followed TA's expedition closely and moved Flat Stanley up Everest through participating in physical activity. TA delivered Flat Stanley back to Woodland and did a presentation for the whole school.

experiencing. Luanne founded the medical clinic at Everest base camp. She was trekking in to help set it up and then do some personal climbing to Camp Two. Luanne walked to Namche with Ang Jangbu who delivered my first post mail of the expedition.

The next day we hiked to Thame for another round of acclimatization. As on the day we hiked to Sangboche, the two women trekkers, Mary and Daphne stayed behind so I was on my own with the guys. The initial pace was brisk, and I kept up near the front of the group for the first several hours. We raced through Thamo without stopping. I had hoped to visit the nunnery since I had had a significant experience there in 2002, but the team cruised through the village without pause. The trail steepened considerably, and I occupied my mind with memories from the last time I had passed that way.

Liz and I had met some Buddhist nuns in Namche. They were asking trekkers for donations for their nunnery because the prayer hall roof badly needed repairs. Most of the nuns had made dangerous journeys over high Himalayan passes to escape from Tibet. We donated to their cause. The next day we decided to hike towards Thame, not realizing that the nunnery was in Thamo. Dawa, who knew we enjoyed visiting Buddhist sites, took us to the nunnery. While we were there, Liz and I put all the pieces together and realized that we were visiting the nuns whom we had donated to the previous day. We were invited to sit in the prayer hall while the nuns chanted. The deep-throated syllables vibrated through the core of my being. Suddenly, I was transfixed. A voice that was not my own came into my head: "Someone needs to tell these nuns' stories. You are that someone. You need to learn to make films."

The beating of drums and clash of cymbals brought me back into the prayer hall. I was shaking. We left the nunnery and trekked back to Namche. I didn't share what had happened to me until Liz and I returned to Kathmandu. There, stranded by a Maoist strike, I typed the words "film school" and "Canada" into Google. A link to the Gulf Islands Film and Television School popped up and I clicked on it. The school had a month-long filmmaking program starting a few days after we were scheduled to return to Canada after a year of travel. Given my experience in the nunnery, I signed up right then to attend the program in September 2002.

After Thamo, the expedition team crested the hill and rested near some stone benches. The break broke my connection to the past and returned me to the present. Some of the team decided to return to Namche, while the rest of us pushed on to Thame. It was tempting to turn back since the hiking was quite arduous, but it felt important to push myself. I found a spot in the middle of the pack where I could go at a sustainable pace. We arrived in Thame after four hours of hard hiking. There was one last steep climb to the monastery. When I stood in front of the Buddha statue on the altar of the prayer hall, my eyes rimmed with tears. I turned my eyes downward in a meditative gesture and felt strength and resolve infuse me from the stabilizing space that surrounded me.

I had wondered if I would receive any new "universal guidance" when I passed through Thamo on the return to Namche. There was not nearly such a dramatic message as the first time, but the lesson I took from the day was to go at my own pace. I tried to keep up with the faster-moving men, but after a few hours I realized that it was not sustainable. It was easy to let my mind run away with thoughts like, "If you are breathing this hard so low on the mountain, how will you ever climb it? You're lagging behind. Maybe you didn't train enough." I reassured myself that my performance meant nothing in terms of the longer expedition, that I was still acclimatizing, and that breathing hard was to be expected.

I calmed my growing insecurity by saying, "I am either fit enough or I am not. I can either get to the summit or I can't. Beating myself up because I can't keep to the front won't help anything. My pace is fine. Everything is OK even if I am last or breathing hard." I kept all of my inner dialogue to myself. I learned on past expeditions that men rarely disclose their inner worlds, and I didn't want them to perceive any weakness in me.

I returned to Namche tired but exhilarated. It had been an important day of pushing myself. I treated myself to a hot shower at the lodge and felt as if the scalding water was washing the doubt down the drain. I called in an audio update to my website and welled up with tears reading some of the messages sent by kids. The final topping on the day was a feed of sushi, my favourite meal. I crawled into the tent satisfied in knowing that I had sucked the marrow out of the day.

A typical trekking day landed us in Deboche. We were up at six, packed by seven, and on the trail by eight. The Sherpa staff spoiled us with tea delivered to our tents and meal after amazing meal. The route contoured out from Namche, dropped down to the Dudh Kosi, and then climbed dramatically up to Tengboche. During the steep climb, I suspected I wasn't the only one to wonder, "If I'm breathing hard here at 3,800 metres, what will it be like at twice that elevation?" When such avalanche of doubts would descend, I reminded myself to just keep taking one step at a time and to keep my view narrowly focused on the trail in front of me. This grounded me in the moment, and I could remember that "this moment" didn't mean anything in terms of "the next moment." Everything is impermanent including big hills.

Fiona Adler, having read my concern about breathing hard on the ascent to Tengboche, was kind enough to share some of her experience. "Don't worry too much about already huffing and puffing at these lower altitudes. It's all relative, and you'll acclimatize as you get farther up. I remember feeling so unfit last year when the Sherpas would whiz by–even though I knew I was fitter than I'd ever been. Altitude has a way of doing that, but just keep plodding at your own pace. One of the guys we were with last year kept saying, 'The training is over now, it's time to focus on staying well.' Good advice if you ask me! I had been telling myself the same thing but it was helpful to hear it from someone else.

Soon after breakfast the next day we headed down trail about ten minutes to the Deboche Nunnery. It housed six nuns, and we made a special effort to visit since it receives far fewer visitors (and therefore less donations) than the Tengboche Monastery. A young nun opened the prayer hall and watched curiously as we Westerners explored the unfamiliar surroundings. I was struck by the Buddhist iconography that adorned the walls. Several times I became teary at its meaning. Since we knew the lama, the head monk and teacher, was not going to be in residence that day at the Tengboche Monastery, several of us chose to light butter lamps, in offering for our safe ascent and descent of Mount Everest. This was an emotional moment for most, for as we lit the small candles, we squarely faced and accepted the dangers ahead.

After lunch, I headed back up to Tengboche on my own. I enjoyed hiking alone because my mind didn't need to dwell on pace. I climbed high above the village to commune with thousands of prayer flags catching the wind. The ridge had several chortens memorializing past lamas of the monastery. The Tengboche Monastery allows visitors to observe afternoon chants. The young monks wore an assortment of modern logo-adorned clothing in yellow, orange, and red. After the conch blew, they quickly came back with traditional robes covering their more modern accoutrements, and they assembled behind the lead monk who swung burning juniper. The aromatic smoke filled the hall along with the melodic chants and mantras. The vibration in the hall seemed to emanate from deep within the polished wooden floor and cradled all who heard the rhythmic syllables. As the day closed, I felt deeply appreciative of having the dharma (the teachings of the Buddha) in my life, and, I suspected from past experience that climbing Everest would provide many more embodied lessons.

Making the jump from Deboche to Dingboche, we left the trees behind. We began the day in a tall pine forest and ended it surrounded by small brushy scrubs and lots of rocks. As a rock wall fan, I admired many examples of Nepali stone masonry along the trek. Absorbing the amount of labour that must have gone into building the walls, yak pens, houses, and lodges was near impossible. Ama Dablam was on my right shoulder for most of the walk. It is such a striking peak that it seems impossible to climb, but I knew that several expeditions make their way up it each season. I felt strong and focused during the entire day.

We camped in a yak pen that night. Higher altitudes meant we saw more yaks. I love yaks. They seem to be a cross between a brown bear, cow, mountain goat, and rhino. They have an aura of wisdom about them–a wisdom born of living lifetimes in cold, harsh places. Yaks belong with saguaro cactuses, icebergs, and redwoods: wise, wise souls that cause me to look deeply inward and outward at the same time; to hear music and silence in the same breath; to taste honey, ginger, and garlic mixed together; to catch the scent of roses and mule dung lingering over a hillside; and to feel both alive and dying in the same instant. The male is called a yak and the female a nak, which makes "yak cheese," which we commonly ate, a misnomer. I fell asleep to the sounds of softly chewed cud and the tinkling of yak bells.

We took a rest and acclimatization day in Dingboche. In the morning I headed out solo again up the valley towards Chhukung and Island Peak. After previous day's high, I had a sense I might struggle again with "pace," so I thought it would be good to reduce the amount of external stimuli. I knew it was time for me to work on "The Climb Between My Ears." I had realized that climbing Everest would be as much an internal process as external. So far the trek to base camp had been an intense internal process. By the end of my solo walk, I succeeded in reducing the amount of chatter in my mind, and I enjoyed drinking in my external surroundings rather than my internal landscape.

After lunch, we ventured down to Pheriche to hear the high altitude talk at the Himalayan Rescue Association Aid Station. We were reminded that it never makes sense to ascend when experiencing any symptoms of acute mountain sickness. The memorial to fallen climbers outside the clinic was another stark reminder of the potential consequences of bad luck or bad decision-making. In that moment, I was so aware that I was walking in the footsteps of many others. I remembered when I was last here in 2002. I trekked to base camp, alongside the Ford All Women's Everest Expedition. I remember being both in awe of the women I shared the trail with, as well as surprised at how "ordinary" they looked. I guess, to the trekkers I passed on the trail, I looked ordinary too. It was still hard to believe that after 25 years of dreaming, I was now actually climbing Everest.

Chapter 9

ILLNESS AND THE ICEFALL

Sickness shows us what we are.
–Latin proverb

During the months before my expedition, I talked to many mountaineers who had been on Everest. I sought their advice and guidance. Almost all warned of the likelihood of getting sick at some point. They gave hints for avoiding "Khumbu cough" and "Base camp Trots." Phil Ershler concluded our conversation saying, "It's not what shape you arrive at Everest in, it's the shape you are at the six-week mark that will determine your ability to climb high." I took Phil's advice seriously and repeated it in many subsequent conversations. I couldn't know at the time how profound his injunction would be.

The first hint came in Dingboche. During our second night there, I awoke feeling nauseous. I endured a few hours outside the tent "dispatching" dinner in a most violent way. I felt much better sans the meal, but wasn't sure if I would be able to move up with the group in the morning. I spent much of the rest of the night playing through various scenarios–mostly telling myself that the light of day would bring the answer. Breakfast was a big challenge, but I managed to get some hot drinks to stay down. At the deciding moment I felt less nauseous, so I elected to give it a go. My duffle was given to a porter so I could turn around at any point.

I knew slow and steady was the way and just put one foot in front of the other. I was surprised that I wasn't too far off the pace since I expected to be bringing up the rear. A few times I ran out of gas and would take a GU to give me the energy to keep going. We arrived at Tuglha for lunch and I managed to keep soup down. After lunch we climbed the Tuglha hill to the memorial chortens for both Westerners and Sherpas who have died in the mountains. The group fell quiet and stopped to take in both the sobering and inspirational sense of the place. Tears rose when I saw Sean Egan's chorten. Like me, he was a university professor in Canada seeking to inspire his students to higher aims. He died at Everest base camp in 2005. The previous year, one of his students summitted Everest in Sean's honour.

After lunch, I was able to stay with the front-runners, though that wasn't my intention. When we reached Loboche, Luanne, our trek doctor, remarked, "TA you kick ass!" It was then that I realized the gift of being sick that day. I could recognize and acknowledge the mental and physical strength

I possessed to gain 600 metres on clear fluids alone while at the same time, reduce my own expectations of myself and that freedom was a gift.

The next morning I was still struggling with nausea. I had to work with my mind and body to eat and keep the food down. I gagged frequently, but I knew it was important to eat. When we left Loboche, my body felt like it was on strike. Though the terrain sloped gently upward, I felt like I was dragging each step from the depths of my soul. It felt very arduous and my thoughts cascaded to wanting to quit. I knew the only thing to do was to keep putting one step in front of another.

We stopped for a break before a steep incline. I took in some GU and wondered how I was going to get myself up the hill. But with some more energy on board the incline fell away easily, and the intensity of my inner world followed suit. From a temporary place of impossibility, great views of mountain summits emerged. It's funny how many times I have to learn various lessons over and over again. On Aconcagua, I thought I had learned the grocery lesson about ensuring I had eaten enough calories, but I guess not. I was also getting glimpses of how intense physical sensations also triggered equally intense emotional states, and I saw one of my major Everest tasks as learning to ride my internal roller coaster.

In the last few hectic months before leaving for Everest, I used to joke that climbing Everest would seem like a vacation. Trying to balance work, training, preparations, and speaking engagements had left little time for much else. In many ways, the trek to base camp was like a vacation. Outside the hours of walking, there was time for reading, card playing, journaling, and taking life pretty easy. The Sherpa staff spoiled us rotten, and their efforts contributed to the vacation-like atmosphere.

We caught glimpses of Everest's summit pyramid and the Khumbu icefall as we completed the last kilometres of the trek to base camp. Usually the group got very quiet during such moments, as the reality of where we were going sunk in. Everyone was excited to be arriving at base camp after two weeks of trekking. We moved into our individual tents and started unpacking our huge duffels. Pemba, the head cook, banged the pots signaling that our first meal was ready. We scrambled up eagerly to the mess tent to enjoy his fine cooking. The temperature plummeted as soon as the sun sank behind the lofty horizon, so we quickly headed for our fluffy sleeping bags. No one stopped to enjoy the remnants of the full moon beaming down on Nupse, one of Everest's sister peaks that towers graciously over base camp.

The next day began with a briefing for summit climbers. It was necessary, but left me wondering if I was skilled enough to be climbing Everest. Throughout the meeting as Mark Tucker, the team leader, detailed his expectations of us, I was pummeled with doubts about my readiness. Mark told us we could be pulled off the expedition for our own safety if we weren't able to climb fast enough. I reassured myself by replaying the conversation I had with Phil in Germany: "Phil thought I was ready, I have trained hard, and I know what I'm doing." Mark also detailed what we could and could not report in our web casts from the mountain. We were not to mention anything but our own climbs. Specifically, Mark warned that we could be removed from the expedition if we mentioned teammates or any bad news on the mountain in our posts.

After the meeting, I was obviously shaken. I met with Mark and Ang Jangbu Sherpa, the two leaders of the expedition. Mark assured me that he had no concerns about my abilities or fitness, and that he was only trying to set a tone of respecting the mountain's inherent dangers. I left the meeting feeling somewhat better but the doubts that that meeting provoked would surface again throughout the expedition. The meeting, as well, triggered an unspoken sense that we were competing with each other; no one wanted to have the slowest time.

I met with Mingma to put my glacier rig together. Using climbing cord, we constructed a series of loops that would connect my ascender and carabiners to my harness. The rig would enable me to connect to the fixed lines that protected the Khumbu Icefall, Western Cwm, and Lhotse Face. With the awkwardness of those newly dating, Mingma and I began the process of learning to work together by practising ladder crossings and crampon techniques. It felt good to be closer to doing some actual climbing and to see how competent I actually was. The day helped me settle into base camp life, and I was eager for the challenges that lay ahead. I was nursing a bit of a cough but my belly had settled down. I hoped I had paid my dues on the gastrointestinal front for the whole expedition, not having any inkling of what awaited me later in the expedition.

I cried myself to sleep that night. I was so tired from night after night of dicey sleep at our new altitude, and a worsening cold had me feeling so poorly, that my emotions from the day began to spill over. I did not fight the tears but tried to sob quietly so my teammates would not hear me. I felt better after the big release and then took some Diamox in hopes of a better rest. Diamox changes the PH of the blood and speeds up respirations so climbers can sleep better. The only problem with Diamox is that it causes frequent urination. I woke up feeling more rested than I had in days, but now my cough was producing thick, unsightly phlegm.

The next day, I felt well enough to participate in a training session on fixed rope ascension, rappelling, and glacier travel. The session was fun and helped me appreciate my mountain skills. While we practised at the base of the Khumbu Icefall, one of Nupse's hanging glaciers let go, and we watched the avalanche flood down the slope, knowing we were in a safe location. Slowly and silently the giant white cloud descended upon us. By the time it passed over, we were covered in spindrift snow.

From our perch atop the ice waves of the lower icefall, we could appreciate how base camp was growing day by day. It was as if the Mother Goddess had sprinkled wildflower seeds over this corner of the Khumbu Glacier. Colourful blossoms were popping up on the ice in clusters any gardener would be proud of. Building a base camp takes tremendous labour. The glacier ice must be pounded into submission and leveled so that tents galore can be set up to house climbers, sherpas, kitchens, communications, and medical facilities. Base camp has its own medical clinic staffed by volunteer doctors.

Since the glacier moves, all structures need continuous maintenance. Each team climbing Everest puts down an environmental deposit that is not returned unless the team properly deposes of all trash and human waste in mandated ways. At base camp, we deposited our "dumps" into blue plastic barrels. Specialized porters hauled the excrement down the valley to villages where it could be dealt with appropriately. Our garbage was also collected, sorted, and taken down the valley to various disposal sites.

On our third morning in base camp, we had our puja ceremony. I felt very blessed to attend since I had read about such ceremonies for years. The lama had arrived from Pangboche the previous night. The entire team circled the puja altar in the early morning frigidness. All were dressed in down parkas and pile pants to ward off the biting cold. The ceremony began with the lighting of juniper boughs to create a thick smoke. The lama recited chants and mantras with four Sherpas sitting beside him. It is not unusual for Sherpa young men to spend some time studying in a monastery.

The altar was a four-foot rectangle made of stone. The top was adorned with five mountain-shaped stones. On the altar, there were sculptures made of butter and tsampa. Tsampa is barley flour and is a staple in the Sherpa diet. Butter lamps, chang (barley beer), mountain snacks, beverages, and katas (ceremonial scarves) also adorned the altar. The lama's melodic chants wafted up towards the wakening icefall, and were carried up and over the hazards by the smoke of juniper burning beside the alter. From then on, before each venture through the icefall, all climbers would circumambulate the altar and burn juniper to ask protection from the mountain's hazards. The smoky air was filled with an atmosphere of both frivolity and the sacred–a spiritual party reflecting both reverence and celebration.

We sipped chang throughout the puja and threw rice towards the mountain whenever the lama did. About halfway through the three-hour ceremony, the puja pole was raised with colourful prayer flags and katas flying in eight directions from the altar. Everyone stirred with excitement as the Lung Ta, which means windhorse, flew sending prayers up toward the Mother Goddess. Red, white, yellow, blue, and green colours presided over every corner of our base camp. Soon after the puja pole was raised, we each received some tsampa to eat, to throw into the air, and to smear on each other's faces for long life, safety, and summit success. At this moment, reverie took over and the tsampa delivery approximated a good-natured cafeteria food fight. Blessings and good wishes were shared all round along with snacks and beverages. More rice was thrown and our team was now blessed, ready, and able to make its way up the mountain.

During the puja, I felt quite poorly. I was nauseated with waves of cold and heat running through my body. At one point, I had to sit down to avoid passing out. I felt weak and sickly. To avoid vomiting, I turned my mind toward home and thought of my sangha, my Buddhist community. As I was sitting on an icy glacier in Nepal, they were beginning their spring retreat. It was the first retreat I would miss since joining the group. As we shouted "ki ki so so," and threw rice during the puja here, they would be doing the same, many kilometres away on the other side of the world. The ceremony helped me bridge the huge distance between us.

I thought back to my Refuge Ceremony, two years previous, during which I had become a Buddhist. I committed to taking refuge in the Buddha, his teachings, and in the community of his followers. As part of the ceremony, I was given my Refuge Name, a Tibetan name reflecting my life path. Moh Hardin, our regional teacher, named me Tsultrim Mig Gya, which means "Discipline Great Vision." I silently acknowledged that the path up Everest would require mountains of both vision and discipline.

After the ceremony, Luanne took one look at me and sent me over to the base camp medical clinic. The doctors, one from Canada and one from Scotland, checked me over. They diagnosed bronchitis, started me on antibiotics, and they ordered me to rest for a day or two and return to the clinic daily for follow-up. I tucked myself into my tent for the day and knew it would be hard to watch my teammates begin to make forays into the Khumbu Icefall while I had to remain in base camp. I reminded myself that the expedition was two months long, and getting well had to be my first priority.

After several days of rest and recovery at base camp, during which I could only watch my teammates have their first adventures in the Khumbu Icefall, the doctors finally said that I could attempt to climb. Following years of imagining the reality of the Khumbu Icefall, the time had come for me to experience its icy flesh. Climbers usually begin the traverse of the icefall in the dark, frigid hours of morning, hoping that the colder temperatures might cement the huge gargoyles of ice in place. Knowing, however, that we had set a goal of reaching only the lower ladders, Mingma and I set off after breakfast. The lower icefall is more horizontal than vertical with ice waves positioned like cadenced surf breaking on a tropical beach. Wave after wave must be surmounted and descended, but each with increasing effort, because of the constant gain in altitude.

The Khumbu Icefall is a horrible, beautiful, unstable place. Glistening in numerous shades of white and blue, frozen waves, from the miniscule to the towering, are woven by time into undulations that threaten to topple and break over us in rhythm with an imperceptible tide. It's as if the gods were laughing when they opened the door to heaven's freezer and spilled cloven icebergs down from the Western Cwm. They land in a chaotic, terrifying heap and then flow like a river's rapid toward the valley below, dropping 600 metres in about a kilometre.

More climbers have died in the chaotic frozen folds of the icefall than on any other single part of the mountain. Climbing Everest from the Nepal side demands that climbers navigate the vast treachery of the icefall at least six times. Prior to each passage, even the most macho climbers grow silent, as they must acknowledge their ultimate fragility. The icefall makes it impossible to deny our mortality. Quoted in Walt Unsworth's *Everest*, Dougal Haston says of the icefall, "One can only go in and hope."

As the fall steepened, it became almost easier, as rhythms of breath and step could be recalled from other high altitude challenges. Prior to this more vertical part of the icefall, I felt deeply humbled by every step and breath. Fixed lines and ladders appeared, and the process of clipping and unclipping my safety tether focused my attention. No longer could I luxuriate in the suffering part of my mind; instead, the terrain demanded every molecule of attention I could give it.

The experience was picking the meat off my bones in the way that vultures do in a Tibetan sky burial. As the icy shards I was climbing cut deep into the heart of my soul, I wasn't sure how much of me would remain. Armed with my German grandmother's stubbornness and strength, I knew the only choice was to continue to step through round after round of the icy knives before me and trust that I would survive the gauntlet.

The climbing got easier for me as the terrain became more precipitous and the horizontal waves gave way to cascading ice. When I could set the unrelenting, objective dangers off to one corner of my mind, this part of the icefall felt like a vertical playpen that was actually fun to negotiate. Ever since I was a child, I've always liked to climb. I started with trees, progressed to the garage, then the house, and eventually to rocks and ice. When we began to encounter the Khumbu's famous ladders, I was more than ready to engage my "inner climber."

The ladders and fixed ropes in the icefall are placed and maintained by a group of Sherpas known as the "Icefall Doctors." They are hired by the Sagamartha Pollution Control Committee to establish the route that all climbers use through the icefall. Each expedition pays $400 per climber for this service. These men risk their lives on a daily basis to help keep all the climbers and sherpas safe. Given the instability of the glacier, once the ice doctors push the route through, they have to constantly reattach anchors, ladders, and ropes and reestablish the route after seracs collapse and bury their hard work.

The first ladder was a "single": a single aluminum ladder about ten feet long that assisted us over a steep section. The second ladder was also a single, this time bridging a narrow crevasse. Ladder Three was appropriately "a triple," spanning a much wider crevasse, classic Khumbu. Sitting there, I captured images with my own eyes and camera that I had seen in pictures for years. I wasn't scared or nervous, just eager to give it a go. I crossed over and back with no crampon snags or near misses. I even felt confident enough to capture the classic shot looking down through the ladder rungs.

After Ladder Three, it was getting warm in the icefall and time to head down. The steep section passed quickly and the horizontal waves again took a toll on my tired mind and leg muscles. We got back to base camp just in time for lunch having spent two hours ascending and one hour descending. After lunch, I visited the HRA clinic for follow-up. The docs were pleased with my progress and the absence of any wheezing, but wanted to see me hack-free in two days or they would prescribe an asthma inhaler. After the big aerobic output of the morning, my O2 saturation level had dropped to eighty but they were not concerned. The humidity at base camp is 2-5 percent so I did my best to breathe through a scarf, and twice a day I hung my head over a bowl of boiling water for a steam treatment.

With the first foray into the icefall successfully completed, several of us decided another acclimatization hike was a good idea. Tim, Al, Jean, and I headed towards Pumori with our personal sherpas. Tim and Al had climbed many peaks together. Al, originally from Newfoundland and Labrador, has lived in Fort McMurray for the past thirty years. Tim hails from the United States. Jean, from Ottawa, filled out the Canadian contingent on the team. Jean and I corresponded by email before the expedition.

We navigated the slippery trail over the glacier heading towards Gorak Shep. At a small ridge, we headed off the well-worn path and took our first break. I suddenly started coughing very hard and began to retch. Several coughing fits later, I leaned over a nearby rock out of sight of my teammates and vomited my breakfast. The effluence bounced off the ground and splattered my boots and pants. I swirled some water around my mouth and spit it out trying to clear the obnoxious flavour from my mouth. I wondered if I should continue with the hike.

I took a GU and thought, "I'll give it a try, I really want to do this." As we began to ascend again, my legs felt like they were moving through setting concrete. But the coughing seemed to settle down as we climbed higher. The going was tough and I began again to have doubts. I felt like I was working very hard for every step and several times contemplated stopping. But I did not want to quit. As the only woman on the expedition, I did not want to show any weakness, so I kept finding step after step in the deep recesses of my being.

At the second break a few hours later, the coughing began again. Soon the retching returned and not long after that, I vomited again. This time my teammates watched. Dawa, Jean's sherpa, offered to carry my camera, and Mingma took a few pieces of clothing from my pack. I was reluctant to give up weight, but wanted to continue since I was pretty sure the vomiting was due to the coughing, not altitude.

I rinsed again and tried to snack a bit. My throat was raw and sore. As we ventured up, the terrain steepened, which was a gift. The sheer slope demanded my full attention, and I was finally able to find relief in a breathing-and-stepping rhythm. I took one step for every inhalation. Finally, my body seemed to have some energy and before long we were standing at Camp One on Pumori's flanks.

What a view! When we looked across the lower Khumbu to the Icefall and the Western Cwm, we became quiet once again. This new perch gave us a clearer picture of the route up Everest and our first terrifying glimpse of the Lhotse Face. The sherpas pointed out many of the landmarks on Everest that we would see on the way up. We snapped lots of pictures and had lunch. I found it hard to find anything to eat, since most items in our lunch bag provoked gagging. I choked down a few items between coughs and we began to head down.

The descent passed quickly but my legs were rubbery and my entire body felt weak. I stopped near the ridge to eat a Clif Bar and hoped I could make it back to base camp. Two hours later we returned to base camp and we told of the amazing view we had of the route. I continued to hack all the way down, and Luanne said she could hear me wheeze without a stethoscope. She started me on an inhaler right on the spot and told me to go to the clinic the next day. I did a few more steam treatments that night after dinner and worried away much of the night. "What if this cough doesn't get better?" kept playing over and over in my mind like a scratched CD.

The next morning I killed time until the clinic opened at 10:00. I was listless and worried. Taking one look at me, Ola hooked me up to the saturation reader. I was at 90 percent. She sent me to take a few laps around the tent to test my body under exertion. My sats dropped precipitously to 68 percent. The docs exchanged glances and I went from anxious to scared. Ola said, "I'm worried. With the big drop in your sats, you might be developing HAPE–High Altitude Pulmonary Edema. I hear a small amount of gurgling in your left lower lobe."

"I'm done for!" I despaired. "She'll send me down for sure!" Ola had Suzanne listen to my lungs and give a second opinion. They conferred and, since I was wasn't in too much respiratory distress, decided to give me another day. They prescribed a new puffer and implored me to continuously breathe through a buff or some other kind of fabric. Ola said sternly, "No exertion. Walk gently and slowly back to your tent and do not get out of it for the rest of the day. Send Mingma back if you have any kind of distress."

I gulped and moved gingerly over the rocky course back to our camp. I lay in my tent wondering if my climb was over and what was happening to my health. "I never get sick," I whined to my tent roof. "This is not like me at all. When was the last time I even had a cold?"

Other than going to the mess tent, I did not leave my yellow cocoon. I read, slept, and sent out my daily dispatch. The questions in my mind continued to plague me, and I wondered if my climb was over before it really began. I continued to cough almost continuously and alternated between optimism and despair. My teammates packed their bags for Camp One and planned to make their first full trip through the icefall the next day. Sadness flowed when I listened to their excited voices all round me as they decided what to take and what to leave behind. I heard lots of questions bouncing from tent to tent such as "What are you sending to Camp One?" "Where are you sending your down suit?" "What kind of food are you packing?" They had to sort their loads into piles to be carried to Camp One and Camp Two. Mark held several orientation sessions on the higher camps and using the stoves and oxygen system.

Throughout the night, the cough interrupted my sleep. "They will send me down today for sure," I thought, as I ventured slowly over to the clinic. My resting O2 sat had dropped to 75 percent but there was very little drop upon exertion. That was good news. After another conference, Ola and Suzanne decided to try to interrupt my cough cycle by prescribing codeine. They had treated the underlying causes of the cough, so this was the next step. Since codeine can be a respiratory depressant, I had to take it during the day and keep myself awake. The docs and I discussed whether or not I should go to a lower elevation to heal. They thought, in their best judgment it made sense to remain at base camp for now.

My clinic visits provided some "girl time." As the sole woman on the expedition, I sometimes enjoyed getting out of the all-male environment. After my check-up, we would venture out of the medical tent to sit "on the beach." Using their puja altar as a backrest, the docs laid a mattress down and we all sat watching the icefall in the bright warm sun. It did feel a bit like being on the beach. Unlike in my team's dining tent, where I had trouble participating in discussions of cars or guns, conversation flowed easily with Ola and Suzanne. I often brought them Swiss chocolate from my stash, and they were grateful for the treat. Base camp living is harsh for all and small comforts are appreciated.

I began to feel woozy from the codeine. I tottered back to my camp and tucked myself into my tent for another long, lonely day. The early morning snow had not allowed my teammates to ascend, so again I spent the day listening to them prepare.

When I asked former Everest climbers for advice, they often mentioned patience. I knew it would be very tough on me the next day when my entire team headed for Camp One. I reminded myself that this was the perfect time to practise the very patience the more experienced climbers spoke of. I reflected on the stretch of obstacles and illnesses I had faced on the climb thus far and recognized that I had been quite humbled by it all. Since in my sea-level life I am not often sick, the experience had filled me with compassion for all who suffer from sickness or hurdles. Each obstacle provided me with a decision-point, from which I continued to choose to climb.

I looked back over the previous two weeks and appreciated how I had hung in despite the lassitude that both illness and altitude bring.

"What will my fitness be like when I can finally climb again?" I worried. Hearing this, I told myself, "You are actually still on schedule with your teammates. Given everything, you haven't dropped off the pace." I sighed and then promised, "However hard I have to breathe, however slow I have to walk, however hard it will be, I know I will make my way."

That evening, as I tucked myself into my base camp home, snow began to fall. Later, high winds and lightning joined the weather show keeping many of us up much of the night. At 4:00 a.m., when there seemed to be no break in the weather coming, my teammates postponed their trip up to Camp One. As I endured another day stuck in base camp, at least I would have company.

When the sun came out later that morning and warmed my tent to almost unbearable temperatures, I thought back to those old CorningWare commercials—out of the freezer and into the oven. This describes life on a glacier exactly. When the sun is out, we're toasty warm or blazing hot, parched, sweating, and can imagine we're at the beach. When the sun hides behind a cloud or drops beyond the horizon for the night, the temperature plummets, and we make a quick trip into the freezer. I chuckled as I imagined myself as a piece of CorningWare from my mother's kitchen, able to withstand great temperature variation and decorated with sweet blue highlights.

The doctors had good news when I made my daily pilgrimage to the clinic. My lungs were now clear and they were no longer concerned about HAPE. They liked how the codeine interrupted the cough cycle, so they suggested I spend another day in a drug-induced haze. My O2 sat improved to 79 percent and didn't drop much with exertion. Ola said I could try a bit of gentle walking at a pace that wouldn't trigger coughing. I hung out with Ola and Suzanne watching the icefall and talking about life in base camp and back home.

I described to the docs how in early spring, as soon as the roadsides are clear of snow, many Newfoundlanders make a pilgrimage to their favourite "gravel pit" to deposit a trailer or RV to secure a spot for the upcoming camping season. Similarly, IMG sent sherpas out to Everest base camp in early January to reserve our spot in the gravelly world of the Khumbu glacier. During the past year, when I presented about mountaineering to schoolchildren, I often showed a picture of our expedition's approach to the north side of Mount McKinley. We traveled up the Muldrow Glacier from its very toe, mounting gravel heap after gravel heap. The students always laughed when I referred to this as "gravel pit camping to the max."

At base camp, all expeditions camp on top of the Khumbu glacier. The glacier is covered in a fine coating of gravel somewhat like hair on a newborn (not soft but barely covering the icy surface). Depending on the temperature, small glacial ponds and rivers are flowing or frozen. Paths of convenience between all parts of camp appear in the rocky surface, but I always had to be on guard for slips and falls. Walking around base camp was not a fun or pleasant experience, but I looked forward to venturing farther afield later in the day after my weekly shower.

By now, the sun had nicely warmed the shower tent. Pemba delivered a lovely bucket of hot water and a cup. I shed my many layers and enjoyed the divine experience of hot water falling over my body. Later in the expedition, the sherpas were able to hook up an on-demand propane-fired water heater and base camp showers became nothing short of heavenly. The luxury of a hot shower amid the harshness of glacier living was the first of many Everest paradoxes.

Another contradiction was the availability of almost simultaneous communication with the outside world. Early in my professional career, I wrote an article filled with disdain about the use of communications in the wilderness. I philosophized about the impact that this emerging technology would have on the experience of living and adventuring outdoors. Now, a decade later, equipped with a PDA and satellite phone, I sent daily dispatches from the mountain to two websites.

Each day, Judy, my communications coordinator, compiled all the emails that were sent to my websites and passed them on to me. I eagerly awaited their arrival and cursed the technology when I couldn't get a connection. I surprised myself by how much I had come to depend on the warmth and care of those messages; they helped to get me through the challenges of each high-altitude day. When, during the long dark hours of night, I couldn't sleep due to altitude or concerns about my health, I turned on the PDA frequently to reread the buoying words that always broke through my lonely fear and delivered hope and inspiration.

Judy also occasionally sent the updates that my teammates posted to their websites. Reading their written words was the only way that I knew that they also grappled with fear or the harsh living conditions. There seemed to be an unspoken rule on the team that such feelings were not to be shared on the mountain.

The next night, gust after gust blasted down the icefall and the unfriendly wind threatened to shred my tent. I witnessed every hour between 8:00 p.m. and 4:00 a.m. when I finally got up to initiate my third trip through the icy maze. I stored my boot liners and socks in my sleeping bag so they would be warm when I put them on. I got dressed and organized in my steadfast tent and headed out into the vicious night. At first, I carried that lovely "bed warmth" until the wind stripped it from me with unceasing accuracy.

The sliver moon hung in the gap over the icefall and the stars seemed brighter than usual. I watched the headlamps of the many sherpas ascending the icefall. It was like a reverse of those ski hill scenes where skiers carry lights as they ski down in the dark. I choked down breakfast and met Mingma by the altar. We threw rice and asked for safe passage in the icefall. The day's light was beginning to filter through as we put on our harnesses and crampons. The route was much more spiked in this time than last since sherpas from many teams had begun carrying supplies to higher camps.

In some ways, this trip up was easier than the first. We covered the distance to the first ladder in less time and I was already more comfortable negotiating this frozen otherworld. Soon however, after doing our initial hourly radio check-in, I noticed my energy and body temperature beginning to plummet. I began coughing so hard that I was retching and close to vomiting. I wanted to continue climbing through the icefall, but I was suddenly profoundly exhausted. I turned us around. As Mingma and I descended, he pointed out that one of eight strands of prayer flags had gotten loose in the wind. About 100 prayer flags danced and snaked and celebrated their new-found freedom whipping to the beat of a hidden drummer.

We got back to base camp and I loaded up on hot drinks and headed for my tent. For the next two hours, I could do nothing but stare at the ceiling. I was so deeply worn out that rolling over took intense focus. I felt very ill and wondered if I was going down the HAPE path again. I noticed solemnly that it was Friday the thirteenth of April. Having graduated from the doctors' care the day before with high-spirited optimism, it was hard to make another appearance in the base camp clinic. When they checked me out, my oxygen saturation level was fine, and they diagnosed "exhaustion" from being sick for nearly two weeks up high.

With me teary and knowing what she was going to say, Ola advised, "It's time to head down to Pheriche for some thicker air and rest." It will be almost impossible to regain your strength up here at base camp." Her prescription: "At least four days of little or no activity in Pheriche; eat lots and sleep more." In my exhausted state, the walk down valley seemed daunting, and I wasn't sure how I would manage it. I took being overwhelmed at the task as a sure sign that I had to temporarily turn my back on Everest in order to have any hope of making a successful climb.

Chapter 10

TO PHERICHE AND BACK

Intuition is really a sudden immersion of the soul
into the universal current of life.
–Paulo Coelho

The hike down from base camp to Pheriche went better than I imagined. With each step down, I felt my cells draw in a big breath, and I imagined them all with puffed-out chests. For parts of the day, Mingma and I were stuck behind some yak jams. Other than the dust they kicked up, they set a lovely pace for my ailing lungs.

After the long walk down, I enjoyed being indoors and feeling the warmth of the yak-dung fire in the dining room of the teahouse. Knowing that my past two weeks of illness began in Dingboche, just over the hill from Pheriche, prompted feelings of irony that I was returning to the scene of the crime to rest and recover. After days of inactivity, I benefited from the reflective thinking that occurs for me when I move.

As I stepped over rock after rock in the Khumbu Glacier moraine, I became aware of the veil that I had been looking through for the previous two weeks. The veil was woven of fine taffeta. When it was held close to my eyes, its presence was barely perceptible. When it moved farther from my face, it formed a thick mask that was both hard to see through and hard to ignore. The weft of its fine weave was the voice of doubt. The warp was the various illnesses. Woven together, they plagued my mind and confidence. I realized that the veil had influenced how I have perceived everything–from the colour of the sky to the steepness of a slope.

Getting on the scale at the HRA clinic in Pheriche, I noted that I had already lost ten pounds since leaving home. Since weight loss at altitude can be a big issue, I knew it was important to eat lots over the next few days. I sent out a dispatch to my website entitled, "The Everest before the Real Everest," and received lots of support from people around the world. Fiona wrote again and shared her thoughts. "It occurs to me that this is not really the 'Everest' before the real 'Everest.' This is what its all about. When people ask me what it was like, I usually say that it was so hard, but not for the reasons that most people would imagine. It's things like what you're going through now that make it tough. Now's when you need strength of mind more than anything else. Don't worry about continuing to train–that's not what you need. Go down valley and read, write, listen to music, talk to people, and trust that your body is getting stronger. You'll be fine–don't worry about what other people are doing, you've got plenty of time." I took Fiona's advice to heart and committed, once again, to seeing everything as part of the path. It was all Everest, every step and every breath. My task, as I had told so many young people in the previous year, was to learn from all of the moments along the way.

During dinner, the innkeeper played music on a CD player. I had not heard tunes out loud since leaving home. He put on some Johnny Cash and I hoped "Ring of Fire" would be one of the songs. It had been my anthem during much of my training. My mind rode the notes out of Nepal and back to St. John's. The previous summer, Paul Cunningham had called me. "Would you come out to Camp Delight and speak to our campers? They are all kids living with cancer and I think your story would inspire them."

I gulped and replied, "Sure, no problem," trying not to belie my feelings. I spent much of the next week stewing over what to say. "What can I say to kids with cancer?" I asked myself over and over again. After stewing for a while, I began to see the metaphoric connections between illness and a mountain journey. I remembered that I had felt ill at altitude many times and could use that as a point of connection.

Early in my presentation, I put up a classic photo of me on my fortieth birthday at 5,500 metres with a swollen face and pounding headache. There were many nods of acknowledgement all around when I said, "Many of you in the room probably know what it is like to feel this way." In that moment, I relaxed and knew the presentation would go well. When Johnny Cash's "Ring of Fire" played during my slide show, everyone in the room clapped excitedly because one of the campers had claimed that song at the campfire the night before. It was a magical moment. I was sure the image of a young man who had lost his hair and with giant scars glaring across his body dancing around the room to "Ring of Fire" would help power my steps up Everest.

"Remember the kids," I told myself. "You are only dealing with bronchitis, not something devastating like cancer." I stopped feeling sorry for myself and made a promise to enjoy the next few days of lowland living. "There are things here you need to learn. Wake up and pay attention. This is part of your Everest," were the words I fell asleep to that night.

The next morning, having just read Paulo Coelho's, *The Alchemist*, I set two intentions: to hike towards Nangkartsang Gompa and to listen to the mountains. As I climbed the hill above Pheriche, I knew immediately that I needed to take a very gentle pace, one that allowed me to breathe solely through my nose and that would not tax me too much. Climbing higher, I kept repeating "Gentle, gentle" as my mantra. I veered off the main trail choosing a contouring yak path to lead me to the lowest hermitage of the gompa. I figured yaks must know how to take the best line.

After an hour of hiking, I arrived at the lower stone retreats. I circled the mani stones three times and explored the site. All the wooden doors were locked, but, despite the whipping wind, I noticed a profound stillness. I had a snack and decided to avail of the stillness by meditating, something I had not done much of since leaving home. There was a small bench of granite and I took my seat there. The Chhukung Valley dropped 1,000 feet below me and prayer flags cracked in the breeze. I knew I was sitting where monks from Pangboche had sat meditating for centuries, and I felt welcomed into the sanctity of the space. I set my eyes six feet out as I do at home, but instead of carpet, my gaze dropped into the wild emptiness of the valley below. The space seemed to be a sponge for my mind, and I soon found myself deep without much thought.

After I finished meditating, I thought about my sangha. I missed them. Because of the climb, I couldn't attend the spring retreat. I longed for the intense clarity that comes from sitting day after day as well as the camaraderie of sharing that experience. I missed spending time with Moh, a Buddhist teacher who had been working closely with the sangha. I learned that the group had performed a lhasang for me the previous week. A lhasang is a purification ceremony in which juniper is burned, similar to the puja at base camp.

While gazing down on Dingboche, I allowed memories of the previous year's retreat to fill my mind. We had gathered at a small camp just outside the city. Small windows in the shrine room afforded views of the surrounding forest, and I had to work to keep my mind in the room. I spent much of the week contemplating taking the Bodhisattva Vow. As part of the Buddhist path, some practitioners vow to liberate all sentient beings from suffering and lead them toward awakening. From a foundation of compassion, a Bodhisattva dedicates her or himself to the service of others. This is a huge commitment, not to be taken lightly, especially since the vow is said to persevere over lifetimes. During a meditation interview, I asked Moh tentatively, "Am I ready to take the Bodhisattva Vow?" He responded with an uncomplicated, "Yes."

I paused, my heartbeat overtaking the stillness in the room, and then found the courage to ask, "Can I take the vow with you?"

Quicker than the space between beats, he replied, "Yes, you can."

I swallowed hard, bowed, and said, "Thank you," I knew in that simple exchange–that my life would change forever. Decision made, I turned my mind to sorting out what I would give Moh as part of the vow ceremony. To symbolize my commitment to placing others before self, I was expected to part with something I was particularly attached to. I took a walk with Susan and quizzed her about Bodhisattva gifts. "What did you give?" I asked her. When she told me, I knew. I realized exactly what would hurt to give and what would truly be the thing to part with.

I drove home and retrieved the small glass rectangle. It was made up of four glass cubes on which I had painted a downtown scene of St. John's' famous "jelly bean" houses. Most artwork I produce, I give away with ease. This piece, however, I had kept because the glass cubes were very hard to come by, the colours made me smile, and I loved all the different ways I could look through it. Giving it away would be hard, but it perfectly filled the role of a Bodhisattva gift. On the Saturday of the retreat, after days of sitting meditation, I changed into fancy clothes and gathered with the other aspiring Bodhisattvas. In a small room, with the other members of the sangha who had already made the pledge as witness, three of us vowed to dedicate our lives and practise to the enlightenment of others.

An abrupt gust of wind cracked the prayer flags overhead and the sharp sound brought me back to Nepal. I left my perch and continued up the hill, weaving amid cliffs and rocks, visiting each level of the hermitage in turn. Some were in ruins; others were hosts to strings of fresh prayer flags. As I ascended, I kept repeating my intention of "Gentle, gentle–go with compassion," and I relished climbing uphill for the first time in weeks. It was as though climbing was a gift instead of a chore. Being on that mountain alone provided me with freedom from the gauze, real or imagined, that I had struggled under since the beginning of the expedition.

I was able to climb at a profoundly slow pace, stopping frequently to really look, and to listen over and over again to nothing but the lonely wind and the hollow sound of my mind exhausting itself. I was tempted to climb all the way to the summit of Nangkartsang Peak, but the afternoon build-up of clouds had already begun, and I knew I shouldn't really push it. But I had had a deeply healing morning on the mountain, and it was time to head back to the valley. On the way back down, I tried to remember and embrace the lessons from the heights.

I spent much of the next day reading in the dining room of the Hotel Himalaya, polishing off four books. Benches covered in Tibetan rugs ringed the dining room, and the walls and ceiling were covered in varnished plywood. At four o'clock, the young man who appeared to do all about the place used kerosene to plunge last year's yak dung into flame. We, in the dining room, were grateful for the heat the burning excrement would soon throw our way, as the afternoon winds blew cold in Pheriche. Don Williams crooned from the boom box. The music and warmth transported me back to the dry heat of Zimbabwe where Betty Maponde first introduced me to the country star as I was learning to master a right-hand drive truck. He was the official musician of our long road trips to return street kids to their rural homes. Liz and I were working in Zimbabwe as international development volunteers during the fall of my sabbatical year that would eventually take us to Nepal.

The candlestick on my table threw off a spirited light. At the appointed time, I wrote my dinner order in the book that matched my room number. I stuck to Dahl Bhat since tradition has it served as all you can eat. Given that my appetite had risen from its high-altitude hibernation, Dahl Bhat was an economical way to feed myself. I have to confess that one of my most favourite things in the whole wide world is a hot steamy towel. Each night, at the Hotel Himalaya in a remote Nepali village, dinner started with such a warm, refreshing treat.

Four days after descending to Pheriche, I packed my bag and headed towards Loboche.

When I started out, the veil had transformed itself into a welder's face shield that dropped heavily into place. It was hot and claustrophobic, and as I took my first few steps out of town, I could hardly breathe. Along with the dark shield, many other feelings competed for my attention: fear, anxiety, stress, and excitement. I reminded myself to breathe and to start walking. This eased things somewhat, and I began to make headway up the valley.

As the climb steepened, I was catapulted into my head and behind the shield. For the next hour, I could perceive only my weakness, fatigue, cough, and fear. I imagined conversations with many of my support team members about how hard it was being; how if I didn't start back towards base camp today, I wasn't sure I would go back; how my training had been all wrong; how I'd peaked at the wrong time; how each step felt so hard. I was really spinning in my head, but I kept stepping. The dark glass of the shield kept me from seeing the reality that nothing was wrong at the present moment; it was just hard to go uphill. I reminded myself that it's often hard for most folks to ascend at 4,500 metres. It's not that I wanted it to be easy, but I wanted to feel strong, resilient, and centered–more like I usually was. Like I had felt two days previously on Nangkartsang.

I searched my mind for reasons for the difficulty and came up with a whole host of explanations. It was as if I hoped knowing the "why" might ease the suffering of that moment. I tried to just feel the angst, pain, fear, and let the feelings wash over and through, trying hard not to feed them or cement them in place. And I kept stepping. And stepping. I reached Tuglha after about an hour, took a short break, and tried to go gently up the Tuglha Hill. My cough was already aggravated, so I knew there was no option but to go slow. I set my sights on a rock, walked to it, and took a standing break. I repeated this over and over again, all the way up the hill. I reached the top, took another short breather, and after reiterating my intention of safe return, left the climber's memorial chortens behind.

Having gained most of the day's elevation, I looked forward to meandering along the edges of the glacial moraine. For a while, the lama who does the base camp pujas was behind me. I heard his deep-throated mantras and the click of his mala (a string of beads used to keep track of the number of mantras said). At one point, he and I locked eyes. I silently thanked him for our puja, fingered the protection cord around my neck that he had blessed, and asked intuitively for some assistance with the morning's suffering. As I continued towards Loboche, the face shield began to dissolve and my mind emptied of its urgency. Three hours had now elapsed and the diamond hardness of the morning had passed paradoxically into memory. I could begin to see that I had arrived here safely, that I still had energy and will to go on, and that everything, including me, was OK.

I got back to base camp just in time for lunch the next day. It was good to be back in my strange home of rock and ice. Pemba greeted me with a hot orange drink and since it was no longer fifty rupees a cup, I downed four cups. Base camp was very quiet because all of my teammates were back up the mountain for round two of acclimatization. When I felt anxious because I was behind them in acclimatization, I kept reminding myself that there was lots of time left to climb the mountain. After lunch, Ang Jangbu handed me a stack of snail mail that I devoured while resting in my tent. Mingma arrived in the early evening. He had stayed with his family an extra day. We made plans to spend the next day resting and organizing, with the hope of ascending the icefall the day after.

Chapter 11

BEYOND THE ICEFALL

Whether you think you can, or that you can't, you are usually right.
–Henry Ford

For my 4:30 a.m. breakfast, I requested one of my favourites, Japanese noodle soup with an egg. It went down okay, but as I was putting the final items in my pack a wave of nausea hit like a tsunami. I barely made it outside the dining tent before propelling breakfast all over the rocks. Not the start to the day I imagined before heading up through the icefall. "Nerves perhaps?" I wondered. I went back inside the dining tent sobbing, wondering if I should call the whole expedition off. I finished my hot drink and packing and Mingma arrived.

I did not confess to my rough start. Instead, I thought I would go up for a bit and see if everything settled. We reached the first ladder in about forty-five minutes and I nearly lost the rest of my belly contents. For some reason I wasn't quite ready to throw in the towel, so I kept taking it ladder by ladder, step by step, wave after wave. I knew I could pull the plug whenever it got too much. About two hours in, the steps and necessary narrow focus of achieving those steps had settled me. At brief standing breaks, I took in some calories. We never stopped for more than five minutes at a time. As we made our way through the "popcorn" section, (a nasty section of very rotten ice), I began to nurture a small glimmer of hope, like the sun that was dancing on the ice, that I might actually make Camp One.

There was traffic in the icefall and I just let everyone on my tail pass through. One kindly German fellow remarked that I was, "One tough lady." I wasn't sure at the time, but by the time we reached Camp One, I was willing to accept his compliment. In the way that we do when things are hard, I promised myself I never needed to climb the icefall again. After the ice tunnel, I radioed into base.

"Where are you?" asked Ang Jangbu.

I turned to Mingma, "Where are we?"

He replied quickly, "The top of the icefall."

I passed on his answer and Ang Jangbu asked a series of questions; "Are you sure? Have you passed under the hanging ice bridge? Have you seen the prayer flags?"

"Yes," I answered to all three. I think my four-and-a-half-hour time to the top of the icefall surprised him. He probably expected much worse, especially since I had been sick.

After we topped the icefall, the sun blazed down. My pace dropped considerably and I did some serious talking to my feet and legs to keep them moving. At one point, I looked up the Western Cwm and thought camp was much farther than it actually was. I was beginning to despair when we came through a large crevasse and I saw the tents. My mind filled with celebration because early that morning, if you had asked me if I would be lounging in a tent in Camp One that afternoon, I would have said the odds were near to impossible.

Soon after arriving, we had a lovely "nutritious" lunch of soup, bacon, and M&M's. Living at altitude tends to decrease appetite and increase nausea, so it's generally considered a victory when food is eaten and kept down. After spending most of the day in a calorie deficit from vomiting breakfast, I knew it was critical to eat. I had a slight altitude headache that I hoped would pass with hydrating and breathing. It was common to feel a headache because of the big elevation gain, but thoughts of high altitude cerebral edema were never far from my mind. The views of the summit, Lhotse Face, and South Col were truly breathtaking and intimidating. As I settled into my sleeping bag for the night, I concluded my daily website dispatch by saying, "The wiring of our brains is amazing because lying here in amazing comfort at 6,000 metres, I can already sense a seed of willingness to perhaps tackle the icefall again. It was five-and-a-half-hours of some of the hardest climbing I have ever done, but being here now makes every second of that toughness worth it."

Gusty winds punctuated the night. Snow, carried on the back of the wind, drifted into my vestibule and pushed against the tent door. When Mingma and I met in the cook tent, the bursts were bitterly cold, so we decided to delay our planned hike to Camp Two. Later, when the winds dropped around noon, it was scorching hot, so we didn't set out then, either. Another big wave of nausea hit me over lunch causing me to lose my meal behind my tent. So spent from the retching, I napped much of the afternoon and awoke to another round of snow and cold wind. I motivated myself to get dressed and took a gentle stroll around our piece of glacier. Even a moderate pace left me panting and short of breath.

Because we wanted to keep our packs as light as possible, I had no books, cards, or journal. With no entertainment or distraction, my mind had way too much time to nurture doubt. It was a hard day of vast temperature and mood changes magnified by boredom and loneliness, a deep valley after the previous day's high. When darkness finally came, I was relieved to conclude yet another day of riding on the high altitude rollercoaster. I drifted off to a fitful sleep and prayed that the next day would ease the nausea that had been my constant companion of late.

The next morning, I managed to hold onto my breakfast despite my body's several attempts to stage a coup and overthrow it. I heaved and retched repeatedly, but somehow the meal remained. We packed and headed out towards Camp Two. The route wove around the ends of several huge crevasses, zigzagging its way through the ice maze. After two hours of hard climbing, we stopped and looked back. The tents of Camp One were right there below us: we had barely made any forward progress. At one steep wall, there was a traffic jam of sherpas carrying loads up and climbers coming down. Mingma and I merged into the flow and I moved myself up the fixed line hand over hand. Passing other climbers was tricky because of the steep, awkward route. After passing several unknown climbers, I looked up and saw the beaming face of Al Hancock, the other Newfoundlander on the mountain. He and several others were descending from Camp Two to base camp. They all gave me high fives and wished me well in my run up the Cwm. After a week of separation, it was good to see them.

After a strong start, my pace dropped again. I repeatedly willed ten steps out of myself, sometimes making twenty, sometimes making five. I started over and over again. Over and over again. Knowing I was stepping in the footprints of legends kept me going. The comfort and ease of a step-to-breath rhythm escaped me. My heart boomed in my chest, racing at a breakneck speed, and given my impatience, I could not find a sustainable pace. I wanted to be at Camp Two, not suffering under the scorching heat and feeling so uncomfortable. I felt like I was the slowest moving climber in the history of Everest. Once we arrived at Camp Two, I noted surprisingly that my travel time was in the middle of the pack. I wasn't too slow, it just felt that way.

Nausea seemed to have taken up residence inside me like an abusive spouse. I kept hoping it would stop hitting me, but except for small respites, it threatened abdominal violence almost continuously. The new gain in elevation made my head throb for much of the day. I tried to breathe and hydrate both away but to no avail. Lying in my tent, feeling so poorly, I hated Everest and wondered why I ever dreamt of climbing it. I was lonely and I missed home. I was not having any fun and I couldn't fathom where my next footsteps were coming from. I wondered if the other mountains I had climbed had been this hard. I didn't think so, but then I remembered hitting a similar wall on Denali. I had cried on that day as well. Tears, falling in torrents like the virginal rivers that mark afternoon in the icefall, brought release and relief on both occasions. I was determined, though, that no one else would see the tears leaking from my eyes. At the time, it seemed smarter to keep my anguish from those around me.

I wrote my dispatch for my website but the technology gods were not with me. After four attempts to upload the text, I changed strategy and called in an audio update. I could not hide the emotion in my voice. Hearing my pain, followers of the expedition sent messages in droves. Each time I read a response to my post, the tears returned. The encouragement, support, and belief in me were overwhelming my doubt and suffering, and the release brought new perspective. I found the courage to imagine continuing the next day.

I spent much of the night trying to sort out why the climb was seeming so hard to me. I gave no blame to the nausea that had been plaguing me or to where I might be in my monthly cycle. The next morning, I awoke to my period. Prior to the start of my menses, I had failed to recognize the hormonal blackness that had been pushing down on me. With the dark cloud now gone, Everest seemed like a much different place. I briefly thought, "It's not fair that I have to climb Everest under the influence of monthly hormones." I remembered that altitude often acts as an exponent for me: it multiplies the effect of emotions and hormones, the higher the altitude, the larger the exponent.

After I sprayed breakfast violently behind the dining tent, Mingma and I took an easy jaunt towards the Lhotse Face. It rises dramatically from the terminus of the relatively flat Cwm. The views of the Lhotse, Everest, and the Western Cwm were stunning. After an hour, we stopped walking at the point where it made sense to rope up to cross the glacier. Mingma pointed out the location of Camp Three, halfway up the vertical wall of ice. It looked almost impassable, so I ask Mingma to tell me what it is like to ascend it.

"Slow and steady," he replied. "Take it very slow. You can do it. I will show you the next time we are up here." I trusted Mingma and knew he had surmounted the face's obstacles many times. I asked him to talk about his past expeditions. In his modest way, he detailed moments from his past four summits. He told me of rescuing a climber who had flipped over at the Hilary step and was caught in the ropes. Without Mingma's help, he would have perished. I made a mental note to pay close attention to everything Mingma did and said. We returned to Camp Two with the Lhotse Face now occupying the number one position on my anxiety list.

The temperature in my tent at Camp Two ranged from minus twenty degrees Celsius at night to plus thirty-nine degrees Celsius during the day.

I tried to hide from the sun in the dining tent to no avail. This was a much easier day and I enjoyed the company of two teammates who had remained at Camp Two to further their acclimatization. My altitude headache turned off and on in response to breathing, hydration, and the amount of ibuprofen I took. My mood was still bouncing around like a yo-yo on steroids, but I seemed to have more slack for the ride. I thought about Pema Chodren, one of my favourite Buddhist authors. She advocates for taking away our habitual escapes such as drinking or television. Pema knows that it can be human nature to run away at the first sign of discomfort. She, instead, recommends "running towards the biting dog." On Everest, it seemed to me, that I was surrounded by not one, but a pack of sharp-toothed canines.

When I climbed Denali there were no escapes that didn't put the expedition at risk for the entire team. We actually did a ritual where we each tied a knot in a piece of rope to signify our commitment to the team and expedition. The entire team summitted after twenty-six grueling days of climbing. I never once had to wrestle with ideas of escape. Everest was a very different experience. Escape was easy and could be enacted in the drop of a moment. The pull of such an easy escape was entering my mind frequently, especially with the frequent nausea and vomiting. I knew I would have preferred the Denali arrangement where I did not have to deal with this kind of mind wrestling.

My cough returned. Mingma blamed it on the Camp One water. I hoped it was just Khumbu cough this time and not a return of the bronchitis. Sleep refused to comfort me that night and I was thankful when it was finally time to rise. Being the ever-optimist, I had high hopes for the morning's nutrition. I got through the meal, but as soon as I bent over to reach for my crampons, I was running for some non-tented real estate to make a violent deposit. I finished and came back to my pack saying, "Breakfast is overrated." This is a long-running joke for me, though more often it is sleep that is overrated. I tried to feel compassion for everyone in the world who felt nausea by using the Buddhist practice of Tonglen. With every in-breath, I drew in my nausea and the nausea of others. With every exhalation, I sent out relief.

I rinsed out my mouth, put on my harness and crampons, and we began descending the awakening Cwm at six. Soon my pace slowed considerably, and I knew I must have used up my liver's glycogen reserve. I braved a GU and some water and eventually each step didn't seem to have leaden boots on the end of it. Just above Camp One, I finally met Paul Adler. He was doing his first acclimatization climb to Camp Two. After months of email, it was great to meet in person in the Western Cwm. I swapped out some gear at Camp One and took a bit more water on board. I was still feeling leaden and weak. The undulations below Camp One leading to the icefall were very taxing. My cough was ever present and several times it was strong enough to bring on more gagging.

We kept walking and reached a part above a very dangerous section of the icefall. Mingma suggested a break and then said, "We have to move quickly and not stop until we are through the danger part." I didn't think I had a quick bone in my body at that point, but I said, "I will do my best." In my weakened state, each step was an individual effort, but I knew there was no other option. It was then that the metaphor of being on a sailing ship came into my head. There I was, feeling queasy as waves of ice rose and fell all around me. I had no idea when an icy wave would slip from its mooring and crash down on my deck. I was sure that many fishers and sailors in Newfoundland had shared that uncertainty.

The path rose and fell, rose and fell. Icy blue towers hung above. Icy blue towers fell below. Mingma and I were caught in a frozen storm that gave the illusion of stillness and permanence, but instead there was terrifying evidence lying all around of potentially murderous movement. I was much more aware of the lethal surroundings than on the way up. There was, however, no practical way to move any faster, so perhaps denial or naiveté was best. Today, I cursed Mingma in my mind because it was such an act of will to make my body move. At the same time, I appreciated his knowledge of the icefall and the times where we could stop briefly in a harbouring spot to delayer and hydrate. At some point, enough calories found their way into my system and I felt like I was able to run down like the wind. I found my flow both in movement and in clipping the fixed lines. I was grateful for my relative ease with the ladders, as we had crossed over thirty of them on the way down.

The photographer in me loathed the necessity for fast travel through the icefall, since there were so many beautiful images to capture in that vast ocean of ice. I snapped a few along the way. When we reached the lower icefall and my adrenaline began to fade, I again had to fight for each step uphill in those last seemingly unfair waves of ice. "This should be easy since we just came down 1,800 metres," I thought to myself. No such luck. When I reached base camp, many of my teammates revealed that they also found those last waves taxing and unfair. I received a hardy welcome back and over lunch I reveled in catching up with everyone's adventures. Talking with the others, I realized that despite having no food on board, I had descended the icefall in good time and form. Unfortunately, I threw up lunch, thus slowing my recovery from the morning's exertions. I hoped to have more luck with a sweet treat from the base camp bakery later in the afternoon.

I managed to keep a freshly baked cinnamon roll and then dinner down. After the big descent, I hit my tent right after supper. I wrote in my journal, "I think I'm coming to understand how women can have more than one child. I was once again swearing that this morning's trip through the icefall would be my last and now a few hours later, the memories that caused that thought have begun to fade. Impermanence is such a powerful concept, and I must grasp it over and over again." I realized that it was Wednesday and I was missing another meditation night at home. I consoled myself with appreciation for all that Buddhism had taught me.

Chapter 12

BASE CAMP BLUES

To know something, then, we must be scrubbed raw,
the fasting heart exposed.
–Gretel Ehrlich

I awoke very early the next day. Steel clouds hung heavily in the sky holding in the night's chill. After dry heaving into my tent's vestibule, I returned to the luxury of my sleeping bag for a few hours. I hoped listening to my favourite music would ease the nausea washing over me in waves. After breakfast, we had a crevasse rescue clinic, and then I luxuriated in a base camp shower. Later, I toddled over the icy rocks to visit my doctor friends at the HRA clinic.

Ola and Suzanne were excited to hear of my high-altitude adventures, but neither of them really had any new suggestions for my current health challenges. Ola said, "It's common to feel nauseated at altitude. Why don't you skip breakfast and try to eat later?"

"But," I exclaimed, "the nausea came on suddenly after I had been at altitude for several weeks. I don't think it's related to the altitude." Somewhere deep inside, I knew the nausea wasn't Acute Mountain Sickness, but I couldn't find the words to convince the docs otherwise. They listened to my lungs and urged me to continue to actively care for my cough with steam treatments and an inhaler.

"Basically, living at high altitude is hard on your body," Suzanne reminded me. "And as a result, life is often hard. Keep taking good care of yourself and hopefully the nausea will pass." The previous night at dinner, Mark, our expedition leader, had said, "Your suffering is really just beginning: Life will get significantly harder as you climb above Camp Two." "Oh goody," I thought. "It's been such a piece of cake so far." I hid from the stiff afternoon wind, bundled into my sleeping bag reading. I started the day quite up and bouncy, but sank as it went on. I was disappointed that the doctors didn't have a way to cure my belly problems or at least have some way to prevent the daily vomiting that was preventing me from putting weight back on.

A sharp crash interrupted my reading. I leapt from my sleeping bag and unzipped the door to see that one side of my tent platform had fallen over. The destruction was evidence of time passing and the glacier moving. That night I changed headlamp batteries for the second time realizing that I had left home forty days earlier; it was the mid-point of the expedition. This was the longest expedition I had been on to date. My previous record was thirty-four days on Denali. It's funny how living in a tent can come to seem like the norm.

Over the previous year, I had wondered what my reaction would be to hearing of a death on Everest while I was on the mountain. I knew I couldn't know until it happened. After breakfast the next day, it was easy to tell that something was up. The important people were standing about with radios, conversations were going back and forth, and many stared up the icefall. We waited. We knew we would be told what was happening when the time was right. Eventually Mark came over and said solemnly, "A sherpa was killed on the Lhotse Face early this morning." The group shrank into silence. Stunned. Not wanting to believe. Mark reminded us not to blog or call home about the death so the authorities would have time for notifications to his family.

There were few details of his death available. We were each forced to stare directly at our mortality. It was easy to drop into denial about the dangers of being on this mountain, and, like passing a car wreck on the highway or hearing of a plane crash, we couldn't help but examine what we were doing there, wonder if we should be there, and remember that eventually each of us will die. It was hard on me not to share my reactions to this inevitable moment with my on-line support team. Considering the dangers of this mountain, I had known it was not a question of if someone would die, but when.

When I first heard, a heavy curtain descended on me. I felt horrible for the sherpa's family. I wondered if he had suffered. I felt like I had been kicked in the gut. Eventually, I learned his name was Dawa Sherpa. Selfishly, I gave thanks that he wasn't on my expedition team so there was some distance from what would have been intense grief, but it still pulled at me. I peppered myself with questions. "Did I somehow contribute to this man's death by being here? Am I comfortable with the sherpas risking their lives so much more than I risk mine? Is this a climbing ethic I can live with? Is this a signal to stop? Do I honour sacrifice by continuing or by stopping?"

These and other questions continued to swirl around in my head. I mentally sent out condolences to his family, friends, and loved ones. I hoped his team would take care of his family. I also transmitted my appreciation and gratitude to our sherpa staff for making the climb possible and for the great risks they undertook on my behalf. On this day of loss, I received a reminder of another loss.

The previous January, a student I was close to passed away. Michael Beecher Smith was a young man with a huge, huge heart. I taught Michael in two outdoor education classes. The loss for his family was immense. I received an email from his mother asking if there was something I could do in Michael's memory on Everest. I didn't know it at the time, but Michael's birthday was nearing, and his family's grief intensified once again. I immediately agreed and asked if they would be okay with me mentioning Michael by name. Once I heard that they were, I began to ponder what I might do.

Michael was on the university's wrestling team and spent lots of time in the weight room. We often ran into each other there and he was a huge supporter of all of my climbs. As a wrestler and weightlifter, Michael knew how to "play through pain." He had to make weight for wrestling, and he was always trying to get me to take my greens and other supplements because I was training so hard. Michael seemed to know when to say an encouraging word or when to come over and tell me to push the bar a little further than I thought I could. He was so excited for me. I had felt his spirit with me several times while on Everest, especially when the going had been so hard. I knew that if Michael were alive, he would have been following my climb daily.

I decided to create a memorial for Michael recognizing his spirit, his heart, and his tenacity in a way that would help me climb both the literal and figurative mountain in front of me. I hiked out about an hour from base camp towards Pumori and Gorak Shep. At a spot called "The Ridge," I climbed off the beaten path to a flat bench of land with a spectacular view. This special spot was on the shoulder of Pumori, which means "Daughter of Everest." I took liberties and thought of Pumori as inclusive of "Son of Everest" as well. This ridgeline overlooks Everest base camp, the Khumbu Icefall, and, when there are no clouds, the summit of Mount Everest. At first, I thought I would build a memorial chorten, but since Michael did not die in Nepal, I came to a different vision.

Michael grew up in Newfoundland and Labrador. The aboriginal people of Labrador use inukshuks to mark paths and guide people along the featureless tundra. An inukshuk is a sculpted pile of rocks that resembles a person. Thinking that we all need guidance and direction, I decided to build an inukshuk for Michael's spirit. As I hauled each rock, I thought of each piece representing some part of Michael's gifts and talents. It was tricky to get all the stones to balance on top of each other. During this time, I thought of Michael's challenges and obstacles. When I put the crowning rock into place and hung Tibetan prayer flags from the inukshuk's shoulders, I thought of Michael's fondness and appreciation of me.

Michael understood that I am happiest when I can combine several passions into one moment. That morning, in Michael's honour, I brought together mountains, teaching, spirituality, and stonework. I'm sure he would have smiled at the combination. After the sculpture was finished, I sat in silence staring in the same direction as the inukshuk. When the time was right, I stood, touched the inukshuk's shoulder, wished Michael peace, and returned to the main trail with my tears falling from my eyes.

While returning to base camp, I was really working hard to make peace with feeling so lousy. Breakfast had been a small dish of yogurt and two small pieces of bacon–nothing else seemed the least bit appetizing. On my hike out to the ridge, I could feel the lifeblood energy bleeding out once again, and so choked down half a Clif Bar. It was hard not to get discouraged as I pulled each step out of the depths of my starving body. I gagged frequently on my walk, and it felt like my esophagus was being turned inside out with each episode. I kept puzzling over what was going on in my body: "I'm usually such a good eater and I have never had such prolonged nausea. What's happening to me?"

After lunch, which remained ever so briefly in my body, the inventor of the "Top Out" mask visited our camp. He took us through the entire system and gave lots of tips for using the mask. I was thrilled that the base mask was quite similar to the one I used with the Go2Altitude hypoxic training system. I had never used O2 in climbing but had enjoyed lots of scuba diving. We were all planning to test out the oxygen system on this rotation up the mountain.

Some of my teammates had been planning to ascend that morning but a part of the icefall route had collapsed. They would try again the next morning. I planned to continue resting and sorting out how to get calories to stay in my body. Pemba surprised the team with a favourite meal, sushi maki rolls. I reveled in devouring and then keeping down several wasabi-drenched servings. "There is hope for me yet," I thought that night as I crawled into my sleeping bag. I started adding sugar to everything and hoped that my body had finally figured out that food is not the enemy.

Winds roared down the icefall for much of the night. At times I wondered if my tent would still be there in the morning. Even so, I slept pretty well and awoke to news that some teammates had headed up. The cold cutting wind made me happy to be staying put. After an uneventful breakfast, I reorganized my Camp Two bag that would go up the mountain. I cleaned up my tent and attended to several mid-expedition tasks such as laundry and refilling sunscreen and drug containers. The wind was so brisk and the wash water so cold that post laundry, I crawled back into my tent to restore my hands to life. I read some of my book, got that lovely drowsy feeling, and took my first nap of the trip. The temperature in the tent was perfect, and I rested deeply and contentedly until lunch. I played about twenty games of solitaire after lunch and lounged about writing my website dispatch. It was a perfect day of taking it easy, after a particularly intense stretch, especially since I spent the day free from nausea. "Sushi cures all," I declared to no one in particular.

Jean and I decided to do our next rotation together. We discussed the merits of going up to Camp One the next day or the day after that. We needed to weigh that status of our bodies, the weather, and when our teammates were climbing. The high winds that morning led us to choose the day after in hopes of a change in the weather system. During our discussion, a major avalanche let go from the West Shoulder of Everest. A collective gasp went up from base camp when it appeared that a long line of people coming down the icefall would be buried by the torrent of snow. Forty sherpas were carrying the body of Dawa Sherpa down from Camp Two. Shouts of relief were heard as the spindrift settled all over base camp, and the black figures on the icefall reappeared. A major disaster was averted when the snow funneled just below the descending sherpas.

I quivered with relief and climbed into my tent to read my daily diet of support messages. They were sustaining me much more than food. I often read them three or four times. Judy pointed out that it was a year ago that I had my first major fundraising event for the climb. It was called "TA's Road to Everest." Even though I had been at base camp for over a month, it was still hard to believe the road actually led here. "I am climbing Mount Everest, I am climbing Mount Everest," I repeated disbelievingly.

The next day was a Sunday. On Sundays I called in audio updates to my website via satellite phone. I wanted followers of the expedition to get to hear my voice on occasion and the audio system was a backup for when the text-based system would not cooperate. I had just returned from a fun visit to the HRA clinic. Even though I had vomited breakfast, the doctors cleared me for acclimatization round two. My voice was about three octaves higher than normal. My coughing had irritated my vocal cords causing them to swell. Suzanne said, "You'll sound like Minnie Mouse until the end of the expedition when your vocal cords get a chance to heal."

"Terrific, " I moaned. "Maybe I will take up opera." The funny thing is that several of my supporters thought I sounded "much better" during this update.

I spent much of the day packing and getting ready to go up the next day. I signed out my oxygen mask from Mark. I planned to carry it up to Camp Two and leave it there for my summit bid. I practised hooking it up to an oxygen cylinder over and over again. Here at base camp, in the warmth of the sun, it was an easy task. When I set up the system for real, it would be much more difficult. I planned to start using oxygen at Camp Three during the summit attempt. I would sleep on it at Camp Three and then use it from there on up. I needed to be able to put the oxygen system together correctly and efficiently, because higher up I would be impaired by both altitude and the severe cold.

I remembered that Paul Adler's summit bid had been thwarted by an oxygen system failure, and the consequences of that could have been much more dire than just losing the summit. Paul had coached me to practise the set-up of the mask many times, as well as to memorize oxygen flow rate and usage tables. I walked around base camp in my mask with the oxygen flowing. What a treat to move without breathlessness for a change. Anxiety for the days ahead rose in my belly. I felt like a hearty game of ping-pong had broken inside of me, with long rallies going back and forth. "You are ready. You can do this. Every step of it," I prompted myself. "I hope the nausea stays away and I have an uneventful climb tomorrow."

My wish did not last long. Dinner became performance art once again. "No big deal," I thought. "I'm used to losing a meal." This, however, was my second lost meal in a day. I fortunately went back to sleep fairly easily. One of the small joys of living in a tent is that I only had to make it past the zipper to throw up in the vestibule. I reminded myself to watch where I stepped in the morning.

The alarm went off at 4:30 a.m. and I made all the right moves for a day on "the hill." Layers on, inner boots laced, pack packed. When I bent over to pull my inner boots into my outers, the morning ritual began and I heaved all the water I had drunk all night out of me and into the tent's vestibule. "No problem," I said confidently. I got my boots on and stepped out into the cold, dawning morning. Unfortunately, this time the vomiting didn't make me feel better. I felt increasingly weak and nauseated. I kept trying to get my ice axe on my pack. Three times I was beaten back by intense waves of nausea. I kept trying but the attacks were too much.

As an outdoor educator I am trained to assess risks. In the inky blackness I told myself to step back and look at the bigger picture. I was now without food for almost sixteen hours, and there seemed little hope breakfast would stick around. "No! Stop. This is not a condition in which to ascend the icefall." These were hard words but necessary ones. I needed to move fast and sharp in the icefall. In no way did that describe me that morning. I was overcome with emotion as I told Jean to go on without me. He hugged me, and I said with my voice shaking, "I am so tired of throwing up."

He answered, "You'll get better, see you up the mountain."

"Tell Mingma I am not going up, will you?" I asked.

"Sure," he said. He turned to go. I listened to the crunch of his boots and I crawled over the vomit and into my tent. I lay in my tent sobbing when I heard bootsteps approaching.

"TA," Mingma called. I unzipped the door and tried to hide my red eyes from Mingma.

"I'm not feeling well enough to ascend today," I said meekly. "I will go to the clinic later and have them check me out."

"I will go with you," he answered. I listened to his footsteps disappear and the tears returned. I called three dear friends for solace and perspective, for in that moment, I felt done. So done. I was so frustrated that the nausea wasn't going away, so sad not to be going on a rotation just then, and so confused as to what I should do. Susan, Karen, and Judy were all good to point out that I had been sick a long time on this expedition and that perhaps my body was reaching its limits. In the dark of that morning, I agreed. "Maybe this is it. Maybe the game is over. Maybe I don't have enough reserve left."

I fell back into a troubled sleep and awoke when the morning sun warmed my tent. I felt like I had been run over by a Mack truck-sized serac in the night. I stumbled out of my tent weak and woozy. Mingma kept a close eye on me as I teetered over to the clinic tent. I sat down on the cot, promptly fell over, and remained horizontal. Ola looked surprised. In the many times she had seen me, I had never looked or acted so sick. She checked me over closely and consulted with Suzanne. After much discussion, they decided it was *Giardia*. They prescribed a two-day treatment and pumped me up on Gravol. I was feeling so poorly at the clinic that we didn't talk future. They gave me the drugs and sent me back to bed. They told Mingma to fetch them if I needed an injection to help keep food down. I returned to my tent and sunk into a drug-induced haze.

With a diagnosis, came hope. "Maybe the drugs will do their work and I can bring my eating back to normal which will bring my strength and reserve back up to where it needs to be," I prayed. In the light of day, I was less clear than in the stark blackness of the previous night. Some hope had snuck in the backdoor and I wanted to give the drugs a chance to work. It was clear that if the drugs didn't work I was probably done on the mountain, as I had already lost 15 percent of my body weight. The general adage is that people who lose 10 percent of their body weight don't summit.

Part of a mountaineer's job description is to make the right decisions over and over again, balancing health, weather, terrain, mountain conditions, and other factors. I often repeated the mantra Ed Viesters used in ascending all fourteen of the 8,000-metre peaks: "The summit is optional, getting down, mandatory." As someone who is generally strong, resilient, and rarely sick, the previous month had been full of life lessons that could only be gained from seeing things from an entirely new perspective. I didn't wish for that new view, but could only do my best to remain open to the understandings and learning that unfolded from the new vantage point.

With the help of the Gravol, I kept a small amount of food and water down and began to feel a bit better. I slept much of the day. Jean and Nat made it through the icefall without incident, and I called and left a message for Jean's wife. The first time he went through the icefall, he asked me to call her. I knew she would be worried so I decided to call and ease her mind. I missed being up at Camp One with my teammates, but I knew I had made the right decision.

When I stepped out of the dining tent that night, the glacier was bathed in translucent moonlight from the almost full orb. The air was crisp and clean, almost pregnant. I stopped to instill the moment in my mind. "There's change afoot," I thought. I awoke at 4:00 a.m. to bootsteps outside my tent once again. A few of the guys were heading up. I had slept solidly for hours and took stock. I felt great. Strong. Clear. Optimistic. Hopeful. Not queasy. "Wow! I feel like myself for the first time in weeks," I thought enthusiastically. "I wonder if I can go up with them? I wonder if Mingma would mind being awakened?" My mind ran away with the hope, and lots of scenarios sprung forth. Again, cooler judgment reigned and I spent the hours before breakfast reading and watching my nylon ceiling.

At about 7:00 a.m., a wave of nausea came and drenched the hope and optimism in a flooding moment. I hung with it, praying it would pass quickly, since I'd felt so well a few hours back. I tried some breakfast and realized too late that I should have had my last Gravol on board. Once again, I decorated the glacier with breakfast. Fortunately, its rocky cover provided good camouflage for my unsightly vomit. I felt immediately better, as before, but then the nausea built again like waves pounding a rocky shore. With each break, I saw my hope sink.

Once the clinic was open, I walked over to secure some more Gravol. The BBC was in base camp filming a second season of "Base Camp ER," so they asked to capture my consultation on film. There in living colour, for everyone in the UK to witness, was me describing the history of my upchucking. The docs unleashed a new theory about high-altitude stomach sphincter relaxation and said, "Keep taking your meds; they'll kick in soon." I visited with the docs for a while and then headed back to my tent. We had an early lunch and I spent the afternoon in a Gravol-infested stupor. Its sedative effect seemed more pronounced than the first day but it was better than the alternative.

Sitting in the relative comfort of base camp, clawing through my mind's haze, I saw there was really no rush to make a decision. It had been a long week in base camp. I finished every book available, played 134 games of solitaire, wished for twenty Vanilla Dips, and rationed out life between feeding attempts and my not so pretty "dispatches." I vacillated between thinking there was lots of time to recover and do a pre-summit rotation and noticing that May had struck. The mountain had been summitted the day before by five sherpas from the North side. I needed about a week for my second rotation, a week to rest, and then another week to try for the top. Of course, that schedule was subject to keeping three meals a day in my belly, gaining some weight, and cooperative weather.

I was in limbo. I was in the "bardo." In Tibetan bardo literally means "intermediate state" and is used to refer to the state of existence between two lives. I tried to remember the Buddhist teachings I had received about how to make my way through the bardo. It was a most uncomfortable spot and one, I knew from past experience, that I despised. I saw no harm in waiting a few days to see what the medications would do or would not do. The worst thing that could happen was losing a few more pounds. I decided to remain in the uncertainty: riding the waves of nausea, hope, optimism, frustration, and drug-inspired stupor. I slept. I drank lots of water. I peed. I ate. I hummed songs from the Eagles and devoured emails of support, care, and love from people all around the world.

That morning in my optimistic state, I wondered about aiming for experiences that might support a second attempt if the summit dream stayed alive when I was back in the low country: experiences such as ascending the Lhotse Face, setting a new elevation record, or using oxygen while I climbed. That afternoon I recognized that I might not recover enough to allow even those. I reminded myself, why, in my expedition logo, the Newfoundland flag was on the 007 rather than the top of the mountain. "This journey is about daring to dream and inspiring others to dream. You have done your best to make it about learning from each step, pushing yourself outside of comfort, and not about the summit as a destination." I was especially touched when one of my instructors from the Denali climb wrote and mentioned some of the tough times I had made it through on that climb. I resolved to keep thinking positively and making decisions each day.

I woke up feeling awful again and sat teary through breakfast. I hardly ate anything and then promptly made my usual morning deposit. It became clear that I was not going to kick whatever this thing was in base camp. Mark dropped by with the suggestion that I go down to recover, and that not all hope was lost in terms of timing and rotations. I said I would drop by the clinic and then make a decision. I walked heavily over to the HRA clinic. Ola was kind enough to listen as I tried to sort my way through all of the feelings, options, and logistics. It was she, a few weeks back, who suggested I go down to Pheriche to recover from the cough. I learned from Ola that *Giardia* could cause lactose intolerance. I had been eating some yogurt to try to support my GI system, so I may have been shooting myself in the foot. The docs sent me to my tent with some probiotic capsules and something else to try to settle my belly. They both agreed that it was time to go down.

I spent the afternoon swirling in indecision about how far down to go. Having had so little nutrition in my system over the past several days, I could hardly imagine walking to the icefall, let alone climbing it. Given this, since my reserves were so low, perhaps I should stop the climb. On the other hand, I knew how much my previous visit to Pheriche gave me new strength and health. I went back and forth. "I don't want to give up too early or easily, and I don't want to be stupid and push beyond my body or mind's limits," I mused over and over again.

I went to talk logistics with Mark. "Can I go down and see what happens?" I asked. "If I don't get better or don't want to come back up, can I be reunited with my gear without coming back to base camp? Or should I make a hard and fast decision right here and right now?"

"We can pack your bags and send them down by porter if you don't want to come back up. We've done it before." I breathed a sigh of relief and went back to my tent to rest and read support messages from my on-line clan.

Our greatest weakness is our greatest challenge. Making this kind of go/no-go decision is always one of the hardest things I ever do. I want there to be a "right" answer and there never really is. That afternoon, I was reminded of a haiku I wrote as an adolescent:

I seek the answers to the questions
When I accept that there are no answers
I will know the answer.

Chapter 13

WHICHEVER OF THE TWO OCCURS, BE PATIENT

Disappointment to a noble soul is what cold water is to burning metal;
it strengthens, tempers, intensifies, but never destroys it.
–Eliza Tabor

My body was cruel. When I awoke the next morning to head down to Pheriche, she threw off the veil of illness and allowed some oxygen to kindle the flame of hope. I felt terrific. Awesome. Strong. In that moment, I didn't feel like I needed to go down. I started to scheme: "Maybe if I did Pumori base camp today and rested tomorrow, I could be ready to go up though the icefall on Saturday." Given my experience of the other morning though, I didn't exactly trust my body. I got out of the tent and sat on a rock, staring up at the icefall, hoping the answer could be found in its icy folds. The morning sun was already hot. It was a fabulous dawn to the day.

I did not want to go down. I did not want to pack. I was at a loss to understand my experience. I went to the dining tent and had some Cheerios and a hot drink. Then my belly stirred, not as bad as usual, but bad enough to remind me of why I had made the decision to go down. "Though I feel pretty good this morning," I reflected silently. I became a high altitude yo-yo once again. "Go. Don't go. Stay. Go. I'm better. I'm not better. Go. Stay." Words hit my mind like an incessant drumbeat.

I managed some hard-boiled eggs and Cheerios. I was convinced I would keep the food because there was no lactose. If I kept breakfast, maybe I could stay. I experienced small rumbles but breakfast took. I noticed that my quad muscles felt like rubber and empty of energy as I walked around camp. "I should go down. Weak quads don't get up Everest safely," I said half-heartedly. I noted that my pants were slipping down. I could drop them down all the way without undoing the waist or fly. "I should go down," I concluded.

I went to my tent to pack. It was different this time. I didn't know if I would return to this nylon cocoon that had been my home for the past month. Everything had to be put in bags–just in case. I didn't want to pack. After each item, I stopped and tears welled up. I kept stopping to ask myself if I need to go down. Each piece of gear brought the same question. It took much longer to pack than usual. I didn't want to go. It seemed easier to lie at base camp in a high altitude stupor and just hope that things would get better. I placed another item in my bag. I cried again. Finally, everything found a stuff-sack home. Some went with me. Most stayed ready to be placed in a duffle for transport. I was so full of sadness I could hardly breathe the thin air: it was as though the grief had expanded in my chest, filling my air sacks with an intensity that was hard to live through.

I had promised Suzanne and Ola that I would let them know what was on the go. I left my pack with Mingma and scrambled over towards the clinic, a path I knew well, to my best friends in base camp. As I traversed the stepping stones over the glacial lake, the BBC guys said my buddies were over at another expedition's camp and they would be gone for thirty minutes. In some ways I was grateful for if I'd seen their caring faces I'm sure mountains of tears would finally have avalanched from my eyes. I asked the BBC crew to tell the docs I'd gone down to Pheriche to rest. I choked out goodbyes to the folks in base camp, and Mingma and I were on our way. It was a familiar trail: we had already walked this way for this same reason. I felt weak. My mind was a scratched record. "I don't want to go. I don't want to go," played over and over in my head.

The punctuation, in most ways, was what made it hardest to go. Was this a comma in my Everest experience? A period? An exclamation point? An ellipsis? For the first hours I walked towards lower territory, my mind was as busy trying to sort out the grammar of my life. I played through scenarios. I felt for clues. I watched my intuition. I wrote dispatches in my head for each variety of punctuation. Every once in a while I broke through the grammatical discourse and reminded myself, "You cannot know right now. Perhaps the best answer for now is the ellipsis."

Mingma and I almost ran down the hill. I'm not sure what was moving him so fast, perhaps it was only "sherpa speed." I felt like I was trying to outpace my emotions. If I walked fast enough, I could outrun the grief that was boring a hole in my chest like an ice screw that protects a headwall. It felt good to move. Movement always helps me process and I soon realized that my mind had given over to the present moment. I had given up the grammar lesson and was paying attention to where each footstep went. We blew through Loboche because my intuition told me that was where I contracted the *Giardia*. We stopped in Tuglha. There I met Mingma's brother, Pemba, who was leading a trek to Everest base camp. I also met Mingma's cousin who owned the lodge. Everyone clucked in empathy at my plight (and perhaps Mingma's).

We arrived in Pheriche in four hours, shaving thirty minutes from our last time. It was a bit like coming home, and Nuru the innkeeper welcomed me back warmly. The downhill hike had left me feeling strong and confident. The few uphill sections had produced rubber legs and stretching lungs. I suspected that some of my information gathering in the upcoming days would center on how my body handled a nearby trekking peak. In order to return to base camp, I needed to be strong enough to go uphill for six hours at a stretch with few breaks. I planned to test my body to see if the *Giardia* had robbed me of that ability for the long term, or if I could nurse it back here at a lower elevation.

Paradoxically, I ended the day grateful for my body's cruelty that morning. The walk down had been relatively pleasant. If I had descended earlier, it would have been horrible because I was so weak. I was truly happy to feel somewhat better, but it did make the decision to come down twice as hard and complicated. It was an Everest sort of day: making the hard call, facing the mountain of feelings about it, and being willing to stay in limbo as I sought more information and deeper healing at 4,200 metres.

Early the next morning, snuggled in my sleeping bag after ten hours of quality sleep, all things were possible: curing cancer, world peace, climbing Everest. Nearing the top of Nangkartsang Peak a few hours later, when I was dragging steps from deep within, cracks appeared in the morning's veneer of optimism. With seven days of rest and illness vibrating inside me, I knew I couldn't just sit still for the day. I felt well enough to try out one of my "tests." I set out for Nangkartsang Peak, which overlooks Pheriche and Dingboche. It houses the gompa I visited the last time I was here. This time I wanted to go for the top and see how my body did.

The summit was 830 metres above me. I started the climb slow and steady. There were a few trekkers ahead of me who often stopped to catch their breath. Because of my acclimatization, I quickly caught and passed them. "Step, breathe, step, breathe," I said to myself, trying to find a rhythm that would work. The climb ascended a prominent spine leading towards the summit. I passed the side trail to the gompa, and memories from my visit to that sacred space flooded my mind. The trail became less prominent as I passed the intersection. "I guess most people turn back before reaching the top," I mused.

I came upon a heart-shaped rock that someone had propped up. I stopped and stared. "A message from the universe?" I asked the mist that had enveloped me. I took a picture of the rock and thought about the tattoo that adorned my right leg. *Courage.* I had courage carved into my leg. Actually, it was the Chinese character for courage. After leading a rafting trip down the Grand Canyon in 2003, I found my way into a tattoo parlor. Looking through a book of options, I knew I wanted a symbol, and I spent some time choosing between truth, courage, and simplicity. Feeling that I wanted to be reminded to be courageous, I left the place with courage permanently etched into my leg. According to the book, the symbolism underlying the character was a person traveling alone in the wilderness. This metaphor touched my heart.

After about ninety minutes of climbing, my pace slowed dramatically. I took a GU and some water. Each step became a struggle. It felt as though all energy was draining rapidly from my body. I reached into some deep well of will to find the ability to lift my leg time and time again. At first, I could take twenty steps, then ten steps. In the end, I had to pause every fifth step. I set a target of a stick or rock in front of me to aim for and tried not to stop until I reached it. The targets became closer and closer. Each step was a hard-fought victory.

The summit was protected by a scramble of boulders. I slowly made my way through the maze and finally saw the swarms of prayer flags flying from the summit. I sat down and pulled Flat Stanley from my pack for a summit photo. Climbing to where you can climb no higher is a special experience, no matter how high the peak is. "Will this be the summit photo from this trip?" I asked the growing wind. It took several tries to get me, Flat Stanley, and the summit captured to my liking. I had a snack and started down. I noticed a storm brewing and didn't want to be caught out in it. The summit of Nangkartsang was about 200 metres lower than base camp. The irony of struggling so hard to reach it was not lost on me.

As I hiked back down into Pheriche, I had another ironic thought. In 2002, on my first visit to Nepal, I spent two months trekking. During that time, I had to take medication for three illnesses: bronchitis, *Giardia*, and gastritis from drinking too much Nepali tea. "At least this time I've avoided the gastritis," I chuckled. Back at the teahouse, Mingma dropped by from Pangboche. He had a bad toothache. "We're quite the couple," I thought. "Neither of us is enjoying eating." He was planning to go down to Namche to have it fixed. I searched the menu for something that sounded appealing enough to eat. I splurged and had a "Mars Momo" with lunch–basically a Mars Bar wrapped in dough and lightly fried. "Anything to get the calories in," I declared to Mingma. So far that day the nausea had been much more transitory and I liked seeing my sense of humour return–it helped keep things in perspective.

One thing that sea kayaking has taught me is that my perception of sea conditions depends entirely on if I want to paddle or not. At 5:00 a.m., when I feel a bit lazy, the ocean waves seem too big to paddle. At 3:00 p.m. the same day, when I've been on the beach all day and want to get off, those same waves seem to be waning and safe to paddle. Having descended from base camp, I was once again aware of the ways in which altitude affected how I perceived my world. Climbing to extreme altitude is a bit like putting a frog into a pot that is heated to boiling. It doesn't notice it's being cooked until it's too late. Like the frog, I didn't notice the changes in my perspective until I descended, and the lens through which I had been viewing my experience became more apparent. I noticed that, for me, altitude was a grand magnifier. I didn't understand how it worked, but it seemed that altitude, or its accompanying hypoxia, magnified emotions, temperatures, conflicts, hopes, and dreams. I marveled in Pheriche at how intense life in Everest base camp was. When I was there, I forgot that the lens of altitude was in place and I took it all so seriously.

Besides being a magnifier, life at altitude is often harsh and uncomfortable. It takes extra energy and focus to do daily activities. I had also noticed on the previous day that my physical coordination got better and better as I descended. Altitude affects our ability to think and to problem-solve. The higher you go, the more challenge there is to push an oxygen-starved brain through its paces. All of this became clearer when I got out of the "hot water" for a time. When I had trained the past year on the Go2Altitude machine, I had the experience of going instantly from sea level to 4,500 metres. When I came off the machine after an hour, it was much easier to observe the altitude-induced impairment.

After Mingma left, I turned my attention to writing my website dispatch for the day. I scrolled through the summit photos and chose the best one to send out. On my PDA, I looked carefully at my face. Despite the joy of reaching the summit, my eyes looked empty and spent. "How much reserve do I have?" I asked myself as the picture beamed out via satellite. The next morning, when I threw up breakfast once again, I ventured over to the clinic to check my weight. I was down another five pounds and feeling very poorly. My confusion temporarily parted, and I made the decision to stop the climb. I packed my bag cautiously to see if the clarity would stick around. It didn't seem possible to heal at this altitude given there was not much left on the menu to eat. Once I vomited a type of food I found it hard to eat that same food again, and given that I had been chucking for ten days, there were not many options left.

The hope voice had quieted to where I couldn't hear it anymore, and the reality of not being at my best was staring me nakedly in the face. "Mount Everest deserves your best," I reminded myself. "No, it *demands* your best, and you don't have that right now." Though I was sure I could have gotten better enough to drag myself back up to Everest base camp, I finally admitted that I wouldn't have the amount of reserve I would need to feel comfortable and confident in going back high on the mountain. I count on that reserve to combat bad weather, extreme altitude, and steep slopes. The two illnesses I faced since arriving in Nepal had peeled off my layers of reserve and resiliency. I had been whittled down to my very core.

For me, persistence is my lifeblood. I am a survivor. I can get through anything. That morning, in turning my back on the summit, I climbed a bigger Everest than the snow and ice-covered mountain in front of me. For once I said, "It is okay to stop. It is okay not to push to the absolute outer limits of your being." I saw that it was acceptable to go home to heal, and live to climb Everest another day. It was okay to do all of this and hold my head high for having given almost everything I had. All of this new territory was like stepping out on a ladder spanning a crevasse bigger than any I saw in the Khumbu.

Although accepting my human frailty was a summit in itself, it still hurt. Grief cut through me like glacier run-off. I paused at the edge of Pheriche to once again reconsider my decision. I stood next to the village's stupa and ran my eyes up the valley towards Everest. "I don't want to go," I repeated over and over. "You need to go. This is not your time for Everest. You've done well, now turn and head down to heal." I circled the stupa three times, captured my grief-filled face on camera, and headed down towards Pangboche.

I walked from Pheriche to Pangboche often awash in emotion. Because I was an anonymous trekker hiding behind my shades, I could allow the raging saltwater to spill over whenever it rose beyond the spillways of my eyes. At times in the hot sun, those torrents threatened to overwhelm me, but by early evening the glacier froze hard, and I felt nothing but numbness in the frigid night. Eighteen months of energy, effort, excitement, focus, and dreams were coming to an end with those downhill footsteps. Suddenly, there was a vacuum–a large black hole. I was no longer preparing to be or being an Everest climber. In this void, churned waves of grief like rancid yak butter. The heartache that had been hanging around the interstitial edges of my being since leaving Everest base camp now had full permission to come into being. The final decision had been made.

In Pangboche, I found Mingma. He had told me to find him there if I decided to come down. He seemed surprised to see me when his niece fetched him from a neighbour's house. From Ang Pasang's house, we talked via radio to base camp via Camp Two and made the arrangements for my bags and flight from Lukla. Ang Pasang was the expedition sirdar. As we left his house, Pasang's wife placed a kata scarf around my neck to signify good luck in leaving, and the glacier dam that was holding my tears in place almost burst. Given, I won't cry in public, I choked my grief back for much of the rest of the day as I sat in Mingma's in-laws place and then at Mingma's place in Phortse.

When I left Pheriche, I actually thought I was going all the way down to Namche. Meeting up with Mingma changed that plan because he said he would accompany me all the way to Lukla. Though it was hard not to let the tears fall all afternoon, there was some comfort in walking with Mingma and his wife and son from Pangboche to Phortse. We stopped by his house for tea and then he took me to Ang Rita Sherpa's guesthouse farther down in the village. In the privacy of my room there, I wrote to the members of my on-line support circle. I was free again to allow the sun to strike the glacier of my heart, enabling the grief to move downhill. I had rehearsed being felled on the mountain by weather and by bad snow or ice conditions. But I forgot to anticipate being sick. This was new territory with lots of learning in being where I'd never been before. I realized that I was okay, that I just hurt, and that, because this chapter of my life was coming to a different close than I anticipated, I would hurt for a while.

I asked those who had been following the expedition to stay with me as I journeyed home. I did not want to be suddenly without their support. I also requested that they share stories of times they had given their heart to a dream and faced a different ending than what they'd wished for. I wanted to be reminded that I had indeed achieved the mission of Everest-007 and should not allow one ounce of shame to cloud my perspective of that.

Since I had left the expedition without a chance to say goodbye to my teammates, I emailed a letter to base camp.

My Everest Teammates,

I imagine on this day, where I have made one of the hardest decisions of my life, that you are at or are heading towards base camp, with only your summit rotation left to go. Having been to Camp Three, you all know how much Everest takes out of you. I respect Everest too much to risk my life and the sherpas' lives by going up without enough reserve and resiliency. Everest will still be there when I am healthy and ready again.

In Buddhism, we speak of Bodhisattvas. Bodhisattvas delay their enlightenment until all beings are enlightened. Though I doubt it works this way, I hope I can be the Bodhisattva of illness for the team. I hope that "I took it for the team"–that none of you comes down with anything that prevents your summit bid.

Rest well and deep my friends. Draw on your courage and strength as you make your last passage up and down Everest. Take good care of each other and your sherpas. Make good decisions. Be safe. Enjoy these moments you've worked so hard for. May you all reach your summit. Please take a piece of me with you as you venture up again. Know that I am cheering for you every step of the way.

TA

Earlier in the day, as I watched Mingma's children play, I was relieved to be heading home to my brother's kids, Rayne and Xander. In that moment, I knew I had made a good decision. I was willing to take risks to climb Everest but not foolish ones. "Your health is more important than any summit," I told myself. I thought back to the morning I had spent building Michael's inukshuk. I realized it was one of the most "right and profound" moments of the entire expedition. That morning I hoped Michael's spirit would help me "do the thing I think I cannot do." In my mind's eye at that time, I pictured the traverse from the South Summit. This day instead, his spirit helped me to do what I thought impossible a few days earlier. Knowing there were times when Michael pushed his body too hard or too far in sports, I chose instead to end my Everest expedition. I listened to his spirit and promised him, "I will come back to Everest again when I'm healthy enough and with enough reserve to face Everest's mighty challenges."

The high-altitude world is one of white, blue, and shades of grey. Whenever I come down from that stark world, I feel as though I am getting my senses back. The next day as Mingma and I dropped in elevation, many colours and textures rejoined the palette. Trees. Leafy things. Thorny things. Flowers. Blooms. Brilliant pink, yummy purple, subdued lavender, powder brown, lime green, spruce green, narrow green, squashed green. Multitudes of living plants adorned the trail. Birds sang. Rivers shouted.

Everest's summit was visible when we got near Namche. I turned and said goodbye, though perhaps the French, "Abiento–See you again," would have been more appropriate. I was almost glad when we turned the corner and I couldn't see the mountain any longer. I had been in Namche forty days earlier. The nausea was still there, flowing more like an undercurrent rather than a raging torrent scouring the creek bed. I did not vomit for the first time in days, though nothing was appealing to eat. I picked away at dinner surrounded by a group of female trekkers.

It was different to see women in greater numbers again. In high-altitude mountaineering, about 10 percent of climbers are women. On my Everest team there were twenty-two summit climbers. I was the only woman. I realized that if I included all of the staff, I was outnumbered sixty or so to one. Given that men and women often process their experiences differently, sometimes I felt lonely on the mountain. I was angry only once on the entire trip. One of my teammates asked his personal sherpa if the sherpas preferred working with male or female clients. He replied that they liked male clients better because "they were stronger." I didn't say anything out loud because he was mirroring many cultures' beliefs, but I sure wanted to prove him wrong.

Like the aftershock tremors that ripple through after an earthquake, I awoke the next morning feeling a bit better and couldn't help myself from running through a scenario. "Pangboche today, Loboche tomorrow, Everest base camp the day after that rest. Go up," I plotted. Then the undulations stopped and reality set in. "My duffels are somewhere in Namche, I'm not strong enough even if I feel better, and that door is shut for now. Grief's like that–you have to accept the loss over and over again."

Mingma and I started hiking down towards Lukla at quite a clip. At the bottom of the Namche hill, we met one of Mingma's former clients. They had summitted together in 2000. He was headed up to Island Peak and Everest base camp with his family. One of his client's traveling companions asked the inevitable question: "Will you climb Everest again?" I had been anticipating having to answer this question, so I took my first opportunity to try out my response. "The easy answer is yes. The short answer is no. The real answer is, 'How can I know right now?'"

As we trekked lower, plywood went by. And glass. And plastic pipe. And corrugated roofing. Coke. Beer. Noodle soup. Carried by men using woven baskets and tamp straps. A few women. Too many children. The Khumbu supply chain was in full swing as the mass of spring climbers and trekkers had depleted the supplies up the hill. I silently thanked each one as they went by for carrying up my food and supplies. As we climbed the last hill before Lukla, we passed the "Everest Summiteers Lodge" and a sign for the "Everest Summiteers Association." Each reminder sent a serac cleaving from my heart–though I reminded myself that even if I stayed 100 percent healthy, I'd still have had only a 20-45 percent chance of standing on the summit. I used lots of soothing self-talk and tried to steer myself clear of all the second guessing my mind wanted to get into. Mingma dropped me off at the guesthouse. We sat awkwardly having lunch and then he asked if he could go. He wanted to hustle to catch up with his former client. We had walked fast again, which gave him the daylight to make a return trip to Namche in one day. With an exchange of addresses and a handshake, he was gone and I was alone in Lukla.

My bags had not yet arrived. I sent a text message up to base camp hoping they would know when the duffels might turn up. The teahouse owner made arrangements for me on the first flight out the next morning. He cautioned I might not be able to fly without my luggage. I wandered through Lukla's one street, not interested in anything. The guards played soccer on the upper runway of the airport. I was sad and listless. I got a cinnamon roll at the bakery, and played twenty games of solitaire, and watched for my bags. I wrote a dispatch for the website and tried to call friends but couldn't get a connection. The universe seemed determined that I stay alone with my grief in Lukla.

A power failure in the evening left the guesthouse in the dark. By headlamp I found my way to my room and hoped for the escape of sleep. I still had no bags. I awoke frequently and stared out my window at the brilliant moon, wondering what I was doing in Lukla instead of base camp. Morning finally dawned and I packed up my sleeping bag on the off chance my duffels had arrived during the night. I went down for breakfast and confirmed my fear that I might be stuck in Lukla for another torturous day of boredom. All the other guests headed across the street to the airport. I sat. Suddenly, the teahouse owner said, "You are going!"

"Are my bags here?" I asked.

"No, we'll send them down later. Quick, you must go now." I ran up the stairs, threw my things into my backpack, and crossed over to the airport. I passed through several security checks then caught my breath in the departure lounge. A windblown man sat beside me. His ruddy face told that he had been up high. He asked, "Are you TA?"

I answered, "Yes. How did you know?" He was an Everest climber who had also gotten sick. He had followed my blog on the mountain. We compared stories and wished each other well in our recoveries. "I'm not the only one," I thought, as I boarded the twin otter. As we taxied for takeoff, I looked out the window and saw my luggage arriving into town on the backs of two porters. I gave a silent prayer for a safe flight as the ground fell away from the plane's wheels. I looked half-heartedly out the plane window and hoped for a smoother flight out of the mountains than in 2002 when I was sure the plane was going to crash. The drone of the engine numbed my mind and, finally, we landed in Kathmandu.

Chapter 14

THE KATHMANDU BARDO

*The true measure of one's worth lies not where you come to be at
journey's end, but in the lives you touch along the way.*
–Anonymous

awoke in a mountain village having heard nothing louder than an avalanche for nearly two months. A quick flight later, I was jarred and frayed and battered by the chaos of Kathmandu. The previous day I had wondered if I would ever get out of Lukla, and now, I wondered what the heck I was doing in this massive city. I was crushed when the person who picked me up from the domestic terminal said that international flights were booked solid for weeks. This was a complication I had not anticipated. The news was hard to hear because I just wanted to be home surrounded by friends. I didn't have the energy to play tourist.

I rescued my bag from the hotel storage and took a shower. It was still quite early so I numbed out in front of the television watching a James Bond movie. It struck me as ironic to be watching a James Bond 007 flick at the end of my Everest-007 experience. After a few hours rest, I walked over to Thamel trying to let the noise, crowds, and pollution wash over me like spindrift. I had lunch at the Momotarou, my favourite sushi place, and had the sense that miso soup cures all. I spent the afternoon with Raj, my Nepali friend. He gave me some advice about airlines and I planned to visit the office of Qatar airlines the next day, once I had my ticket in hand. Raj and I found a much cheaper hotel on the outskirts of Thamel, called the Blue Diamond. As I walked back to the Hotel Tibet in Lazimpat, I realized I had already settled in a bit. My tourist survival strategies were kicking in: I had toilet paper in one pocket and small rupees notes in the other because vendors could rarely make change.

I crossed Kantipath, a major street, in the same way I had crossed the Khumbu Icefall–in the company of Nepalis. I "caught a lift" by walking alongside other pedestrians, since the "horizontal" seracs come fast and furious and merely crossing the street is a potentially lethal proposition. Back in my hotel room, I dug into my new reading material and tried to surrender to the idea that I might be in Kathmandu much longer than I wished. I recognized that I was in transition once again, from a simple life in a tent to an urban hotel in a chaotic city. My duffels arrived from the airport, and my teammates sent down the picture of a rose one of the cooks had drawn with get well wishes. It was hard to imagine them freezing at Camp Two while I sweltered in Kathmandu. "Was I really just climbing Everest?" I asked myself.

I moved to my "downscale" hotel room early the next morning. For a significant reduction in cost from the Hotel Tibet, I now had hot water only when the sun shone, a fragrant musty smell, and access to the movie channel when the neighbourhood wasn't on brownout. I had watched more movies in the previous twenty-four hours than in the past eighteen months. Raj had his wife take me over to Qatar Airlines in Durbar Marg, about a twenty minute walk from Thamel. They had no sign out front of their office but we deciphered the puzzle and took a number.

The middle clerk seemed quite helpful, but I drew the one to her right. No matter what question I asked her, she kept saying, "No seats in May or June." She sent a message to Toronto asking how to upgrade my seat since there might be a slightly better chance of getting a seat in a higher class. I was supposed to check back the next day. I asked her about buying another ticket.

She said, "No seats." I asked her about standby. She said, "No seats but you are welcome to try." As Rupa and I walked back to Thamel, I tried to work hard with my Buddhist slogan for the day: "Abandon all hope of fruition, i.e., going home."

I spent the afternoon aimlessly wandering around Thamel until I wilted at about three. I realized the energy drop was a legacy of the *Giardia*. I began to slowly introduce food groups to build back strength. It felt like I had been in Kathmandu for a month, even though it had been just a day and a half. I retired to my room for a late afternoon nap, early dinner, and more distraction from the movie channel.

The next morning I made my pilgrimage to Durbar Marg. I got the same woman, though she was more helpful this time. Toronto replied, and for a relatively small upgrade fee I could have a seat on a plane in slightly less than a week. I was hoping for something sooner, of course, but I grew instantly lighter. I was still so weary that I thought the universe was giving me time and opportunity to build up the strength to go home. After another afternoon of rest, I had an early dinner and returned to my room just before the lights went out.

They killed the lights at exactly six. "Oh yeah," I remembered. "Rotating brownouts. It must be Thamel's turn for the early-evening shift." I sat in the dark paying attention to the notes of humanity coming together into a cacophony of night. Someone was sawing by hand. An incessant rhythm. A large dog barked, his jowls seemingly vibrating up to the fourth floor. Horns bleated. And honked. And thrilled. The saw paused then went back and forth again. Its beat was punctuated by the staccato lowering of the metal protection gates over storefronts. Some stayed open, making light with their own mini-generators that sing like cicadas. Others called it a night.

Beep. Beep. Honk. Drivers made their way home over darkened streets. Suddenly, with a deep rumble, the hotel started its massive generator, and all the other sounds must now compete for my ears. Voices combined with a bicycle bell. Air hissing overrode other dogs' efforts. It would be a while before the night settled enough to let me sleep, but I had light and TV now which made the night music harder to hear.

Eight hours later, I awoke. The birds were singing like this was the only time they would even be heard. Mourning doves cooed. Songbirds sang. The first horn. The first motorcycle. Wheels began to wake. The chaotic din rose from the quiet as the sun tracked higher in the sky. The huge dog started in again. Nothing got by him. His friends tried to keep up in an effort that could only be called capitalistic. Dog eat dog. Only one can be top dog. Voices joined the fray. Metal gates announced their unemployment in rapid succession. Another day in Kathmandu was born.

Krishna, Raj's brother, picked me up at 6:30 a.m. so we could beat the bus crowds for our "small trip south of town." I often don't really know what I am getting myself into. The first river I rowed on in a raft was the Colorado through the Grand Canyon. My first Himalayan mountain was Everest. So I wasn't surprised when our small journey took us hours up into the hills surrounding Kathmandu on quite a bus ride.

At the bus park, we found a direct to Pharping, but there were no seats left. "No problem," I said, since I didn't think we were going far. In Nepal you don't need to travel far for it to take awhile. Being Saturday, many of the folks in the bus were headed to their home villages or to the same place we were going. The bus tout kept encouraging us to fit more and more folks into the bus. Eventually, I was propped up between Krishna and another man in an intimacy that elsewhere would be reserved for partners. I could not move my feet and was hanging on to the two bars hanging from the ceiling.

The road was not wide enough to let two vehicles pass while moving so the bus jerked forward then stopped frequently. On each hairpin turn, we were caught by vehicle exhaust in a noxious game of diesel-fume tag. We arrived after about ninety minutes, and I didn't trust my legs to move me through the throng to the bus door. We'd given the bus folks something to talk about, as it's not that common for Westerners to ride local buses. Many eyes stared at me during the whole trip, and I was glad, as usual, to have had the experience of being a visible minority.

Pharping is one of the places in Nepal where Buddhism and Hinduism come together. We first visited a Buddhist enclave of monasteries built there because Padmasambava, an early Buddhist teacher, had meditated nearby in a cave. Typically, the community was built on a hill. We climbed the stairs between the various prayer halls, the monks looking older as we got higher. The first temple was dedicated to both Green Tara (Buddhist) and Ganesh (Hindu). Here, the novice monks' voices broke and they sounded like they were chanting out of tune. Two other temples also shared deities in a cooperative juxtaposition that, I think, is rare in religion. The enclave was silent except for the monastic music vibrating from the prayer halls. I was once again enthralled by the monks' deep-throated chants punctuated by cymbals and horns. One older monk invited us to see a temple that had 1,000 statues of Buddha and 1,000 chorten statues lining the inner walls.

We headed next to Dakshinkali, a Hindu temple two kilometres down the road. This was where the crowds were heading. The atmosphere was respectfully festive–somewhat of a cross between the sacred and a county fair. Leading down to the temple were stalls offering food, children's trinkets, flower leis, and animals to sacrifice. Kali is a Hindu goddess appeased by blood. During the fall festival, many animals are sacrificed to quench Kali's thirst for blood so she won't need to cause car accidents or other disasters. I learned that if an individual or family is in trouble, they can appease Kali any day by making a sacrifice at this particular temple. Depending on a person's caste, they would choose to kill a chicken, pigeon, goat, or buffalo. Vegetarians can sacrifice a coconut.

The line to get into the temple to perform the ritual was probably a thousand deep, and folks waited two to three hours in line. Given we weren't participating, we entered via the exit to observe. The temple is near a river, and the animals' feet are bathed there so it will allow itself to be slaughtered. People wishing to appease Kali can kill the animal themselves or pay a person in the temple to do it. There are butchers just outside to attend to the carcasses. People can light butter lamps in the temple in similar practice to Buddhists, and Hindus seem to ring bells in the temple in ways not unlike spinning a prayer wheel.

We rode back to Kathmandu with a few sacrificed chickens. For once I felt reasonably safe in a Nepali bus, because I knew Kali had received as much blood as she desired on that particular day. There were still a few drop-offs that caught my eye and my breath, though, especially knowing there had been two fatal bus accidents in the previous two days. The ride back was even slower because the roads were more crowded. I was wiped out by the travel, but it was exciting to get out of town and see the amazing juxtaposition of Hinduism and Buddhism.

When climbing Everest, motivation can sometimes change moment to moment. I heard more than one climber mention the Rum Doodle at base camp. The Rum Doodle is both an imaginary mountain of 40,000.5 feet and a Kathmandu restaurant icon. Everest summitteers eat free at the Rum Doodle for life. Given my bad luck, I thought I might have to forego the free meal this time round. Anne, an acquaintance from Minnesota, just back from guiding a group to Everest base camp, looked me up and asked me to join her group for dinner. I suggested the Rum Doodle not knowing Anne would pick up the tab. The Rum Doodle's walls and ceilings are covered with "yeti feet." Each twelve-inch foot details an expedition or trek. There are also spaces on the wall where Everest summitteers sign their names. The place gives off a sense of history and the food was pretty good to boot. I appreciated the bathroom signs: one door was labeled "For those who sit," and the other "For those who stand." Some of the women in the group had trouble choosing since they'd just spent a few weeks squatting.

The next day I spent a significant amount of time at the internet café. It was the first day I felt ready to check in on my expedition mates and other Everest climbers. Enough time and emotion had passed that my curiosity won out. The internet is slow in Kathmandu, but I could get the gist of what was happening on the mountain. There had been a summit attempt that night that had been turned back by high winds. "I think I may know how some of those folks feel," I said to myself.

I hadn't vomited in a week and could now tolerate a much wider grouping of foods. I couldn't tell, however, if I was gaining weight yet. I still had transitory nausea and was not eating nearly as much as I usually did. My energy seemed to go off and on like a faucet. Some days I had lots of spunk, other days hardly any. There wasn't any pattern to it, so when energy allowed, I explored. When it didn't, I read or watched movies. I was still counting the days until I was able to return home, but I found my "Kathmandu Legs" and had settled into Thamel. I intentionally chose outdoor restaurants, since it was likely to be much colder and stormier back home in Newfoundland.

I awoke very early the next morning. Steel shutters still lined the streets while I searched for breakfast. Street children remained curled like fetuses on concrete wombs. Their naked, calloused feet told of the miles they walked in search of daily survival. Their tattered, filthy clothes clung to them like old friends. I slipped quietly by feeling a tenderhearted sadness for these boys and the many others forced each day to the mean streets.

After breakfast, I sat in Raj's office. The marketing signs in the window framed the old man perfectly. He sold singing bowls. His face seemed caved in by his years. He caressed a brass bowl in his weathered hand and struck it with a mallet to start the vibration. To nurture notes, he lovingly ran the handle of the striker around the rim. He heard the music. He hoped the riveting note would draw in someone with money. No one appeared to hear. Pedestrian traffic, motorcycles, and a few cars wove between him and me in the rutted, broken street. No one stopped to listen. He played another bowl. I was sad again.

Later, I decided to get brave and have a haircut. Never has someone cut so long and removed so little hair from my head. I chose a place that had a colourful brochure, figuring they must cater to Westerners. I dropped in and asked how much for a haircut. The rate was reasonable, so I said, "Sign me up I gotta clean up this mop before heading home." The haircutter was busy giving a Thai massage so I had to wait. "No problem," I replied, "Time is something I have lots of at the moment."

Eventually, the nice young man looked over and asked what I wanted done to my hair. I explained that I just needed it trimmed up nice and neat. He said that the hairdresser is only used to long hair, that short hair is tricky, and she would have to see my hair before committing to cut it. I tried to explain that I wasn't fussy, that a mountaineering team member once hacked it off with a Swiss Army knife, and that I would be fine with whatever happened. The woman arrived and agreed to shorten my hair. It seemed like she was quite frightened by my wavy locks, so I tried to give her many positive looks. It turned out that she trimmed off less than a centimetre but it must have been a big change because I got catcalls from men all day.

When they were giving out persistence, I was at the head of the line. Bargaining skill, however, I must have missed altogether. In cultures where prices are not fixed, I flounder. My shyness comes out and I prefer to look from afar. Sometimes I can get into the mood and make a game out of it and form a relationship with a vendor. In Thamel, I always tried to go back to the same stores so I could survive the purchasing process. I went back to the hotel with a few bags of souvenirs to find homes for in my duffels. Heading up to my room on the fourth floor, I took the stairs to my room two at a time for the first time since arriving in Kathmandu. My strength was returning. It had taken almost ten days at lower elevation to begin to get stronger. "I wonder how long it would have taken at high elevation?" I mused.

The next morning I began my day of "lasts." I had my last outdoor breakfast at the New Orlean's Café, my last sushi at the Momotarou, and paid my last visit to my favourite bakery. In each place, I bade farewell to the folks who had been dishing me up my recovery diet. I'd been mostly visiting Asia in my culinary choices: Thai, Japan, and India: variations on rice and veggies. I still had no appetite for protein. I packed my bags, got my shoes repaired, and picked up some shirts I had made. I had a hot shower. My hotel room only had hot water when it was sunny. At Everest base camp it only made sense to have a shower when the sun had warmed up the shower tent. My bathing regime had been dictated by the weather for the past two months. I thought, "Wouldn't it be interesting if more of our daily routines were shaped by natural rhythms even in urban settings?"

I took Raj and his family out for dinner at Fire and Ice to thank them for their hospitality. As we parted company outside the restaurant, Rupa and Krishna placed katas around my neck and wished me good travels. Raj was picking me up in the morning to take me to the airport. After a night of restlessness and fitful sleep, it was a relief when the alarm went off at 4:15. I dragged my huge duffels down the stairs quietly and loaded them into the car Raj had hired. The trip to the airport was swift, as only vegetable sellers and joggers were out. We ended up at the airport too early and so we stood beside the dusty road drinking tea in the dark until the guard let us past. The first of six queues had already formed. It was a swirling mass of humanity: tourists with big bags and carts, a family or two, and seemingly hundreds of Nepali migrants heading to the Middle East to work. We stood unmoving for about thirty minutes; then the crush began and people pushed towards the entrance. Carts got relegated to the back as the lightly packed migrants charged forward.

I finally got through to the front. Raj quickly placed a kata around my neck and wished me well. I waved to him, threw my bags through the x-ray machine, and submitted to my first of three pat-down searches. Given women were outnumbered at the airport ten to one, I often made good progress at these stations since they used same-sex security people for the task. The lineup for departure tax was next. Then the lineup to pay Qatar Airlines too much to take my extra bag. Then the queue for immigration. The metal detector. Another line for hand luggage x-ray and inspection.

The last queue was hardest. For many of the migrants, this was their first experience in an airport. The last lineup was for the bus to the plane. As they opened the doors a crack, the crowd crushed forward, not seeming to understand that our seats were reserved–this was not like a bus. I was pushed and shoved and almost picked up off my feet by the mass of humanity flowing through the small opening. One last pat-down search and I took my seat on the plane.

Suddenly and unexpectedly, I was hit with a rash of emotions. I was sad to be leaving Nepal. I was grieving leaving the mountains just as summits were beginning to happen. I was angry and frustrated by the airport experience. I was tired from no sleep. Given some privacy, I'm sure I could have had a big cry. Like a stormy sea crashing up against the Cape Spear shore, I sat with wave after wave of emotion. Then I settled. Settled into the seat I had worked so hard to get. Into the travel mode of patience and bardo. Into beginning the transition home and out of the Everest experience. Into my post-Everest life and whatever it would hold.

Chapter 15

AFTER EVEREST

The bruise on the heart which at first feels incredibly tender to the slightest
touch eventually turns all the shades of the rainbow and stops aching.
–Erica Jong

Adventure narratives always seem to end suddenly to me. It seems as if the author runs out of steam in telling the story chronologically, and by the end they just want it done–the book and the adventure. Four months after leaving the mountain, I feel as if I am still plodding along its slopes. My mind is never far from Everest and I climb it every night in my dreams. Perhaps, if I can just find the magic door in my nocturnal wanderings, time will reverse and the climb would have a different outcome or I won't feel so lost. The ending is so lame. Felled by *Giardia*. Where's the satisfaction in that? No parades, no ticker tape, no fanfare, just solid, conservative decision-making. I don't see the expedition as failure, but I still rail against how the movie finished. No Hollywood ending. No storybook ending. No tragic ending. No ending at all, really.

Roll the edge. Set down. Refill the roller. Roll the beveled edge. Slide the clapboard down. Roll more of it. Refill. I have a bit of extra mind space spared from the task at hand to think of other things. The rhythm of the roller takes me back to Everest and unfolds a deeper understanding of what happened there and since. Climbing Everest was not just the two months I spent on the mountain; it was the eighteen months prior and, most likely, will be the eighteen months post. Though I have been down from the mountain's flanks for longer than I spent there, I still struggle to understand the nuances and meanings of my Everest experience.

It feels as though the mountain is still pushing out against my pores, stretching my skin to almost breaking. The mounting pressure aches through my bones and soul wishing for escape, as do I. Filled to bursting, glacial melt breaks through the dams that hold my tear ducts closed. I cry instantly when any warmth reaches the deep, icy-cold void that sits just behind the mountain. I am both full and empty at the same time, another paradox in the journey.

I stopped writing when I returned from Everest and started renovating. It wasn't that I didn't have things to say; it was just that I didn't know how to say them. My house, neglected through three years of training and mountaineering, called out for attention and I decided to listen. I wanted to create a lovely workspace in which to write this book, so I started with a small plan for the living room. As is often the case with renovations, they spread throughout the house like a bad virus inflicting chaos and stress because the list of necessary work got bigger each week.

In a flash of reflection, I recognized that renovating the house was a process of reclaiming my space and life from the unseen remaining grips of my marriage. Given some of my interactions with Liz during my return from the mountain, I had to finally accept that there was no hope for reconciliation, and I endured another chapter of grief and anger. With each paint stroke and nail hammered, I tried to deal with my backload of feelings. I always expected that there would be a "post-partum" time after Everest, but I hadn't anticipated it being multiplied exponentially through rekindled grief. Without Everest before me to give focus and meaning to every moment, I am lost. Drifting at sea. Feeling as though I've moved backward and am in the midst of the divorce again–though with all gains of the mountain path wiped out.

The post-climb depression is as deep as a dark crevasse on the Khumbu, and I can't yet find the best way out. I could chose the next Everest, but I'm still too tired and depleted from the prior one to know what it might be. I wonder about continuing to live the model of intense adventure that has kept me grounded over the past three years. There was also a big valley after Denali–though it passed more quickly because I listened to the puffer fish's call to bike from Lhasa to Kathmandu and began training again after a month of rest.

Given my mission to reach out to youth, I feel as if I always have to put a positive spin on the climb. There is rarely a situation that lets me share the truest and hardest parts of the entire experience. It's hard, in a sound byte, to convey the vast complexities that were overlapping in my head and body during the climb.

I dreamed recently that Paul and Fiona Adler worked at Memorial. I asked them how they managed getting leave from work for their Everest expeditions, and they said it was easy and that the university understood. This brought great relief to me. As I write I realize that I'm carrying some sense of unfinished business. I'm disappointed in how I've come home. I cut myself slack for the first few weeks, but I'm saddened that I continue to struggle.

I also dream I am dying. Almost every night, dark shadows come to murder me or some dread disease stalks my life. Occasionally, an avalanche crashes down burying me alive, or I fall wedged into the icy tomb of a crevasse. I used to awake in sweat-stained terror, out of breath from trying to escape the clutch of my nightmare. Now I just look the lurid drama directly in the face, remind myself that I am actually dying, and roll over and go back to sleep.

As I biked the next morning, the image of fire came into my mind. I thought of how fire consumes and purifies, of the phoenix rising from the ashes, and how disappointment is like a pile of cordwood. It's hard to burn a log on a smouldering fire. I saw that I came back from Everest with my inner fire dimmed and sputtering. It was tempting to throw lots of fuel on it immediately to get it burning bright once again, but I had the sense that it needed to burn low for a while, with embers gently glowing against the dark night. Everest humbled me. I expected it to. Everest split me open along the midline like the finest surgeon. I expected that too. Everest's snow and ice acted like a polished mirror reflecting my frailties and strength with frightening clarity.

I can see now that it would be impossible to return from such an intense experience with grace and ease. The mess of emotions that I have been untangling were inevitable and impossible to sidestep. Like most crevasses on the Khumbu, this passage required the patience and wisdom to know when to proceed and when to wait, when to step over carefully and when to leap, when to stay silent and when to share.

MAY 2007

From the moment I stepped out of the customs hall at 2:00 a.m. into the arms of waiting friends, I received a wonderful welcome back to Newfoundland! I was touched that friends and people I had never met stayed up late into the night to greet me as I stepped off the plane. The next morning, during a radio interview, the host asked me which I thought would be harder to recover from: the failed climb or the *Giardia*. I was quick to point out that I don't view the climb as a failure. From the very beginning I had been adamant in not tying "success" to the summit. I designed the climb's logo with the Newfoundland flag on the 007 rather than the top to remind me (and everyone else) that "it wasn't only about the top." Of course, there is still much disappointment about not getting a chance to try for the summit, but "failed" isn't one of the words I use to describe my Everest experience.

As I was returning home, some of my teammates were climbing towards the summit. My thoughts and prayers were with them for a good climb and a safe return. I so wished I was climbing with them, but I consoled myself with the knowledge that when and if I was going back, I would return with more confidence and experience. I started uploading my expedition pictures to my computer and realized how many memories were contained in each image. I saw in the pictures that climbing through the Khumbu Icefall changes a person–or at least it changed me. It marked my convocation between Everest trekker and Everest climber. The baptism of those terrifying, beautiful, icy hours changed me from someone who dreamed of climbing Everest to someone who had climbed Everest; from someone who twenty-two months previous could hardly speak the dream aloud, to someone who shared the climb with thousands of kids and adults around the world.

I saw in that moment that *Giardia* and bronchitis could not steal that change or those moments. They could not take away the glory of traversing the Western Cwm. They could not erase staring up the Lhotse Face to a summit that was so close and so far at the same time. They could not alter a communion with people around the world who shared my dream and the hardships of living it out. They merely kept me from climbing as high as I wanted to.

As I transitioned home and shared stories, I began to speak aloud, rather than write of my Everest experience. Using my spoken voice helped me access different parts of the experience and begin to understand it in new ways. I saw it as a tapestry that I will unwind from the loom of my spirit and soul for the rest of my life, knowing that how I viewed its weave pattern will change over time and distance. I did an interview for NTV news. I met the reporter on the top of Signal Hill. It was my first trip up there since I returned, and I found looking out at the city and ocean catapulted me into a reflective state. The memories of hours and hours of training came flooding in, especially as I looked east towards Everest. As I struggled to find the words to answer the reporter's questions, I could almost "see" Everest in the distant clouds. I was still feeling inarticulate in speaking of the experience, since I was just beginning to give it voice. Although I wrote of it daily, I think speech and writing must come from different parts of the brain and each accessed different parts of the experience.

The night of the interview, six of my teammates summitted Everest. I was thrilled for them and ached for me. I was into the part of the transition that was much less fun. The sparkle of returning was replaced by the tarnish of sorting out living back in the "regular" world. I locked myself out of the house. My car mirror got kicked in. I had a "noisy water line" that makes it sound like water is running in the house all the time. The car battery was dead. And because no one banged pots to tell me that it was time to eat, I kept forgetting to. I saw that, in many ways, life on Everest was simple and easy. Sleep. Walk uphill. Eat when Pemba knocks the pots. Read. Sleep. Repeat. Life "on the outside" seemed much more complex and difficult. Funny to notice how my perspective changed with location. Once again, I realized that I was charged with going slow: "Bistante, Bistante," as the sherpas would say, "Slowly, Slowly!" I needed to remember to breathe. To remember that everything is impermanent including transition and I was sure that, quite soon, I would be ensconced in life at home again.

When I called my niece, Rayne, soon after returning to St. John's, she asked me some questions about the climb, and then I queried her about what she had been doing. A little later in the conversation, she said, "You only made it to Camp Two."

I answered, "Sometimes we don't get to climb as high as we want."

After pondering for a minute, she replied, "Did you see the picture of Everest with the heart on top I painted for you, on your website?"

I said, "Yes."

After a few more moments where she was obviously mulling something over in her mind, she declared, "Maybe next time I will paint it shorter so you can get to the top." I melted on the spot and tears streaked down my face.

Four more of my teammates summitted. One had to turn around because of exhaustion. Another had to return to base camp before reaching Camp One because a gastro-intestinal infection had weakened him. I imagined that base camp was awash in a multitude of feelings. I knew some of what the climbers who had to turn back were feeling and sent messages of care and comfort to their websites.

During the May long weekend, one can bank on rain for sure and snow as a good possibility. This year, though, it was gently warm with a grey-blue overcast sky. The city was quiet because most businesses were closed. Many folks were off at cabins or visiting family members. Still trying to reconnect with the place I lived in, I took a stroll down Duckworth Street, one of two parallel roads that form the core of downtown. Off Duckworth rise hills that I frequently walked up carrying a heavy pack as part of training. Each residential street sprouts the colourful saltbox houses that cuddle so closely together they appear joined as one.

I realized that the pots hadn't been banged in a while so I headed up to Moo Moo's for a long weekend ice cream treat. The bovine decorated shop that makes its own creamy treats in flavours like "Newfie Fog," "Turtle Cheesecake," and "Green-Eyed Chocolate Monster," sits atop a confused configuration of streets known as Rawlin's Cross. I stepped into the store and saw that I was not the only one who lusted ice cream; the line was long enough to provide plenty of time to make the big choice between all of the offerings.

A young man was just ahead of me in line. He asked, "Have you gone on your trip yet?" I answered, "I'm just back." He told me I spoke at his school and that I had told the story of how, when I was first training for Denali, I hadn't been a runner. I started off running one minute and walking one minute for twenty minutes. Eight months later, I ran my first half-marathon. He said there was something in that story that touched him, as he had always gotten down on himself for not being a runner. After the presentation, he began running with a more compassionate view, and he explained that he had lost thirty pounds, was running eight kilometres a day, and had committed to running the Tely Ten. I thanked him for telling me of his journey and congratulated him on taking on his own Everest. It was a good day to hear a story of a positive impact the climb had beyond my sphere.

Another four of my teammates summitted. A doctor friend gave a listen to my cough and thought it was viral and would pass quickly. I was worried that I hadn't totally cleared the bronchitis infection while in Nepal. After a few more days home, my sleeping hours returned to normal. Transition has always been one of my nemeses, and even though I had given myself so much practice with it the previous two years, I knew this one, because the experience was so big was bound to be a doozey. Not only was I leaving the mountain, I was leaving the eighteen months of preparing for the mountain behind. The "Road to Everest" leading to the climb had been as full and intense as my mountain experience.

The last of my teammates stood atop Everest, fifteen in all. Seven, including me, were denied that high perch. Feelings abounded as I observed the last weeks of the Everest season from home. I felt like I was suspended over one of the big crevasses in the icefall. I was on a ladder looking down into a large abyss. I was actually quite safe on the ladder but it was dizzying to look down into all that space. One of my favourite sayings is, "This too shall pass." I knew that one day, I would wake up and be off the ladder and on the other side of the crevasse. Until then, I would clip into various literal and metaphorical safety lines, place my crampons carefully, and move from rung to rung with intention and care.

I was sitting in my favourite chair, hitting the refresh button over and over again hoping to see news of Paul Adler's summit bid. Paul had been instrumental in my being able to send updates from Everest. I followed his climb the previous year and had been following the current one closely since

I returned to Canada. I hoped the winds would stay down and he would have a good climb. All of my body parts were crossed and I frequently glanced at the prayer flags I have hung around the house. I was sending out blessings and energy for his safe climb and return. I waited with my heart beating rapidly for hours. Finally, "Hooray!" Paul is on top. I cry tears of joy and relief for him. Now he had to descend safely, so I keep my vigil until I see that he is safely back to Camp Four.

The next morning I did a newspaper interview and spent several hours seeing colleagues and sharing stories from the mountain. Having had more chance to speak aloud about the experience, I was beginning to feel more articulate. I started to feel a bit better physically but recognized how much muscle mass I had lost on the mountain. I went out to get some new pants for a corporate presentation I was doing and the new ones were six sizes smaller. I started surfing around looking for other mountains to climb. Bolivia seemed to be calling me or perhaps the North Pole. Maybe another attempt at Everest. I knew that looking for the next adventure seeds to plant was part of my transition process. I was just browsing. Just looking, like a kid with the Sears Wish Book in November. Flashing through the colourful pages of options. Making a list but no decisions. Just watching where I was being led.

I knew it was too early to make a plan. I needed to rest. As I walked around Quidi Vidi Lake, where I usually run, I noticed how deep the fatigue was. It was time to honour the exhaustion with rest and recovery. I needed to rebuild the reserve and enjoy moving slowly without a yellow pad of to-do lists and training goals. I continued to look at the photos from the expedition. I noticed the hard edges of the Everest experience were already being softened by a tenderness. A tenderness that allowed some thoughts of trying again. "Some day. Some way. No hurry. It will still be there," I consoled myself.

The morning when I landed home at 2:00 a.m., there was an email in my inbox from Lucy by 9:00 a.m. She organizes "Becoming an Outdoors Woman" (BOW) workshops here in Newfoundland and Labrador. She was desperate for someone to teach the hiking and backpacking workshop the next weekend. Literally, just getting my feet on the ground, I said I would let her know by the end of the day. "How can I say no to Lucy?" I thought. BOW is a program that teaches introductory outdoor skills to women. This year was the tenth anniversary of BOW in Newfoundland and Labrador, and I remembered, at the previous year's workshop, being sad I would miss the big occasion.

When the women heard I was coming to lead the backpacking workshop, they were a little worried and intimidated about how hard I would make them hike. They had no idea that, since returning from the mountain, I had been doing more napping than hiking. Along with leading the workshop, Lucy invited me to do an Everest presentation. I whittled down my pictures from 900 to 300 but didn't really sort out what I would say. I let the group know that I was only home a week, so they'd be getting a raw, unpolished version. People who hadn't seen me in a year were startled by the amount of weight I had lost.

I started off showing the film my friend Greg made the previous January to give the audience some sense of my training and intention in climbing Everest, and then let the pictures run and just said whatever came to mind. The audience asked thoughtful questions throughout. I was very moved by the standing ovation at the end of the presentation. It was amazing to see the Khumbu Icefall on the big screen and see the women's reaction to it. Having explained that I had mortgaged the house to make the climb possible, the women jumped up after the presentation to tremendously reduce my inventory of expedition T-shirts and carabiners. I was also awarded the proceeds from the 50-50 draw and signed many autographs for the participants' children. Their support was very touching. We have a tradition at BOW of doing Tarot readings after the day's activities are done. A year previous, when I asked the question of whether the money would come through for the expedition, the cards seemed to lead in the direction that it would. Now twelve months later, I could see that it came through enough to make it possible to go, and I would work to retire the rest of the debt in the coming months by doing more presentations about the experience.

After being home ten days, I was back playing hockey. I worried how hard my first game might feel but quickly realized that I must still have some extra hemoglobin on board. I expected to be quickly out of breath, given the pace of the game, but due to my altitude-induced blood doping, I was able to keep up to the play. It was so good to be back worshipping the puck. When I tripped over the blue line, I thought, "Now I'm in a different kind of icefall." I was also aware of a freedom–the freedom to be injured. There was such pressure during the previous year not to get hurt while playing, or to try to recover from injuries quickly so as to not have much time off from training, that it was a relief to not be pressured by such high stakes.

There was an iceberg off Blackhead. I couldn't remember an iceberg that close to town in several years, so Susan and I drove out to Blackhead and walked along the East Coast Trail to get closer to it. I realized that I would not have seen an iceberg this year if I had been able to stay on the mountain. I took note. I was needing to acknowledge the gains from being home early. I had also been able to attend some very important events in the lives of family and friends.

In early June I was at the side of a dear young woman in my life watching Takunda Trevor Mutseyekwa join this world. Leonorah took on a big Everest challenge five years ago when she journeyed from Mutare, Zimbabwe, to St. John's Newfoundland to begin studies at Memorial University of Newfoundland. Tears flowed from my eyes at the miracle of baby toes. In many ways, the first week of Takunda's life was like a mountaineering expedition. Go to bed early. Awake in the fresh night just beyond midnight. Find the way in unfamiliar territory. Know that a team is stronger than its individuals. Don't sleep much. Steep learning curves. Joy. Pain. New views. Sleep. Eat. Burp. Poop. All that we were missing was the climb uphill part.

At the age of seventeen, Leo left her family and friends and country to begin a journey of learning and exploration that rivals any Everest climb. Now five years later, I hugged her on stage at her university convocation and was at her side when she gave birth to her beautiful son. One afternoon, as I drove to the hospital to visit Leo and Takunda, I heard a radio interview with my teammate, Al Hancock, the first Newfoundlander to summit Mount Everest. I was surprised by the level of grief that washed over me as I listened to Al describe his experience of summitting, but I comforted myself that I was able to be in St. John's to bear witness to other kinds of Everest summits.

The same week Takunda was born, I returned to presenting to children. I gave a slideshow at St. Matthew's Elementary. Many of the children and staff had followed along on the climb, and they had some very excellent questions about the expedition. I knew I would continue to evolve the presentation, but for first go, I was pleased. It was different doing the talk without a Hollywood ending and where the audience knew the ending, but I appreciated beginning to share some of the amazing things I learned along the Everest path.

I received an email from someone named Monica: "I am still reading and enjoying your wonderful writing. You write so well. Glad you made it home safely. Please, keep writing." I was touched and noted the interesting timing, as I had just decided to sign the contract that marked the beginning of my next Everest, writing this book. My goal was to have the first draft ready by mid-autumn so that it could be published in time for the next Everest season. I knew I needed to "buckle down," as my mom would say, and keep writing. It was time to stop surfing around looking for new mountains to climb and, instead, find the words to bring "My Everest" to print.

I was originally scheduled to return to St. John's on June 8th. A few of my friends believed I wouldn't truly settle into being back home until the original arrival date had passed. The transition out of my eighteen-month Everest journey had not been the smoothest, as I struggled to find my way through the large void that remained. It was tempting to fill the void, but, instead, I chose to sit with the emptiness, revel in moving slow, waste time left and right, and obsess about whether or not to replace the Omamobile.

Six months after Flat Stanley left Woodland Primary School, he gave up his wandering ways and returned home. The energy in the gymnasium was electric as the children filed in and took their seats. After setting up the projector, I visited "The Wall." On the wall was a scaled painting of Mount Everest with many other references such as the CN Tower, the Eiffel Tower, and Gros Morne. Using physical activity credits, the children had worked Flat Stanley up Mount Everest. Judging from his current position, Flat Stanley had reached the South Summit, and was making the final traverse of the Hilary Step, and would likely reach the true summit after another session of physical activity.

Woodland Primary is a Kindergarten through Grade Three primary school. After Mrs. Stoodley asked me to take Flat Stanley along on my Everest climb, the entire school got behind my effort. They held a "Pajama Day" where all the kids got to wear pajamas to school and brought a contribution to the climb. I was so appreciative when they presented me with their fundraising efforts. The eager children were treated to a special presentation that included all of Flat Stanley's adventures in training for and climbing Mount Everest. They loved seeing his picture, and during the question and answer period many questions were asked about his experience. After the students asked me about my favourite moments of the climb, they asked about Flat Stanley's favourite moments. They asked if he had fun, if he was scared, and whether or not he might try to climb Mount Everest again.

Several classes requested autograph sessions, and after the assembly I spent some very special time with Mrs. Stoodley's third grade class so they could see and touch some of my mountaineering gear. The crampons were a big hit. One of the Grade Two classes presented me with a spike from the Newfoundland Railway. Judy and I took Flat Stanley out to Tim Hortons for one last Vanilla Dip. Flat Stanley was not sure where his next Vanilla Dip was coming from given his separation from the Queen Mother of Vanilla Dips. I still wasn't feeling very well and had been tempted to postpone the trip to Woodland until September. When I saw the faces of the children, however, I was filled with tremendous pride and gratitude, and I thanked Judy for pushing me to go.

Near the end of June, I started teaching intensively once again. It was useful to have something to throw myself into to distract me from the grief. Having a structure and demands on my time gave a grounding rhythm to each day. I established a routine of getting up early each weekday morning to write for two hours before heading into the office. This gentle discipline provided a container for reflecting and processing my Everest experience. As I cleared the fog of high altitude from the forefront of my perception, each word that hit the page helped me see the experience with more clarity.

Having wrapped up my intensive summer teaching schedule and house renovations, I surfaced for a breath of air as August began. One of my teammates, Nat, sent me a CD with his expedition pictures on it. I looked at the pictures with a paradox of emotion running through me. When I looked at Nat's summit-day photos I was filled with such joy that it all came together for him, with pride in knowing that I now knew personally about forty people who've summitted Everest, and with deep sadness and disappointment in how my own climb turned out. Seeing the pictures reminded me of what I didn't get to see. I had, of course, seen those same images in books for years, but I wanted to drink them in through my own eyes.

The disappointment changed and morphed and ebbed and flowed. Some days I was sad I didn't get to see the curvature of the earth; other days the South Col. Some days I wished heartily for the sense of completion that summitting brings, and others I was filled with appreciation for all the gifts that stopping the climb early had delivered. Some days I did not even think about the mountain; on others, it was all I thought about. Like the acclimatization process, I went up, I breathed thin air, I came down and recovered. I did it again. And again.

I continued to write for a few hours each morning making good progress on the book. Writing the chapter about the decision to stop the climb was excruciating, as I was forced to relive each agonizing moment of that time. I realized how hard it was to share the disappointment with those around me. I chose, instead, to stay quiet or focused on the positive side of things. But, alas, like life at altitude, the full gamut of feelings was all there under the surface whether I shared them or not. Even though I was safe at home, life still felt at the edge, a life where lessons unfolded almost with the certainty of tides.

At the beginning of September, I flew to Edmonton to surprise my grandmother, Oma, for her nintieth birthday. She was touched and very appreciative. From Oma I inherited my sweet tooth, wiry hair, and dogged determination. She possesses a silent strength that is woven through her being and has seen her through many trials and difficulties. Like me, she is a prankster and uses humour to cut the edges from sorrow. While I was on Everest, I thought of my Oma often and tried to tap into her strength and perseverance. I recalled memories of her carrying fifty-pound bags of cement as she neared her sixtieth birthday. Up until she moved into her latest apartment, she used to take the stairs to the fourth floor several times a day. I hope I am half as agile and active as Oma is when I reach ninety. As Oma's family and friends gathered around her, I filled with gratitude for the many significant adults I had in my life as a child. Like her, they helped shape and support me as I grew to adulthood. I hoped I could return the favor to the generations that follow me.

With the approach of equinox, I sensed the change to autumn, both inside and around me. Fall is my favourite time of the year and I appreciated the reflective nature the season invoked by the colourful changes. With more time off the mountain, I gained larger glimpses of meaning and understanding about the experience of preparing for, being on, and coming home from Everest. I came to see how, like the grieving widow, people did not know what to say to me. Instead, a gaping silence was left when they noticed my sadness leaking out from the crevasse in which I tried to hide it.

I reached Camp Four with the book and began to plan a public fundraising event about the climb. As I prepared the presentation, reordered the images, and changed the focus of the narrative, I was finally released from the intense grief that had been weighing me down. I began to emerge from dark, icy depths into the light of day having traversed the post-Everest landscape rife with paradox. I came to see that something can be a crushing blow and a gift at the same time, that going down can push me harder than climbing up, and that sadness and joy can exist in the same moment. I nurtured a budding appreciation for the experience despite the pain in gaining it.

In October I started to train again. "Fall down seven times, get up eight." This is a Japanese proverb that came my way on a tear-away calendar. Of the 365 sayings that year, this one stuck in my memory. One morning, as I ran intervals on Signal Hill, I thought about courage. It takes courage to begin. Whatever I am beginning. A new job. A big task. Changing a habit. Making a speech. Climbing a mountain. It takes courage to take the first step, to overcome inertia, to make it happen. As I progressed up the hill, completing interval after interval, I thought, "It takes even more courage to begin again." To go at something a second time or fifth time or twentieth times, takes much more courage. To overcome disappointment, discouragement, shame, or failure requires a bigger dose of bravery.

Liz always said, "TA, you have to do something twice, because if you only do something once, you can regard it as an accident." When I parachuted out of an airplane, she said I should do it again. When I had a Big Mac after ten years of vegetarianism, she bought me another. Each of those second attempts required more courage than the first, because I knew what it took to do. I knew the horrible terror of letting go of the airplane, dropping into freefall, and the aftershock of the chute opening, all within 5 seconds. That knowledge demanded greater courage from me to be willing to experience it a second time. But, I also knew the immense joy of flying under canopy, and that provided the motivation for walking through the fear again.

Having spent nearly two years of my life preparing for and climbing Everest, I know intimately, the huge emotional and financial costs of such an endeavour. Equally, however, I recognize the triumphs, growth, and inspiration of living so close to my edge. I know now that I want to return to Everest. There are things the mountain still has to teach me, and things I must learn before returning to its flanks. My internal fire is gaining strength once again. I sense that it is time to stoke its flames to new height in order to completely incinerate the cordwood of disappointment and transform it into the ash of possibility. I must rekindle the courage to begin again.

This is my Everest.

ACKNOWLEDGEMENTS

*At times our own light goes out and is rekindled by a spark
from another person. Each of us has cause to think with deep gratitude
of those who have lighted the flame within us.*
–Albert Schweitzer

I am filled with gratitude for so many people. I want to thank them for their support, love, and encouragement throughout this amazing journey. Without them, my road to Everest would have been a tougher one to negotiate, or more likely, I may never have ventured down it at all. The risk in acknowledging people in this format is that I will inadvertently leave some of them off the list. I apologize in advance. Please know I am grateful to each and every person who contributed in any way to me reaching Mount Everest, whether they are mentioned here or not.

First, I want to thank my parents, Heinz and Denise, for their love, patience, and ability to set worry aside so I could follow my dreams. They nurtured my strength and determination by supporting my many passions from climbing to judo to photography to waterskiing.

My Oma and Opa, Frieda and Alois, for teaching me to begin, and begin again.

My brother and his wife, Michael and Shawn, for raising two delightful children, their unwavering love and belief in me, and sending amazing care packages.

My niece and nephew, Rayne and Xander, for sharing wisdom beyond your years, and giving me the best reasons in the world for coming home safe.

My first love, Liz, for your love and support in overcoming obstacles that might have stopped me from growing into the adventurous woman that I am today, and for sharing my first views of both Denali and Everest. May your life be filled with love and joy.

My Zimbabwean daughter, Leo, for your courage and determination to climb your own Everests. May you find your way to happiness and marvel at the amazing road of parenthood.

My buddy, Karen Warren, for sticking with me through Everests of all kinds, for being my writing advocate, and your wisdom, witness, and wit. Meet you on the porch.

My Buddhist personal trainer, Susan McConnell, for answering hundreds of questions about the Dharma, providing lojong slogans for each adventure, participating in post-lojong high altitude training at Bianca's, and being my muse.

My friend, road trip queen, and communications coordinator, Judy Cumby, for all that you did to make Everest-007 a reality: hypoxia babysitter, feeding me, taking photos, postcard sponsor, presentation set-ups, decorating the wall, middle of the night airport pick-ups, strategy sessions, Vanilla Dip Timbits, and most of all, for your generosity in all forms.

My friends and first sponsors, Deborah Bourden and Wilma Hartmann, for their belief in me, marketing mentorship, meals whenever I show up at their house, and the support and expertise of their company, AppleCore Interactive. I can truthfully say, "I couldn't have done it without you."

The young people of Newfoundland and Labrador for inspiring me to inspire you. I hope you will always be physically active and follow your dreams.

My employer, Memorial University of Newfoundland, for its flexibility, support, and participation in making Everest more than a mountain.

My grad slave, Earl Walker, for doing everything from gear checks to glossaries with humility and kindness, and for delivery of Vanilla Dips on a regular basis.

My friend and Kathmandu guardian angel, Rajandra Dahal, for welcoming me and caring for me so well every time I come to Nepal.

My body-care team, Janine Clancy, Hong Lui, Shanna Stone, Renee Albrecht, and Bobbi Sidel, for their generosity and care of my body, putting Humpty-Dumpty back together again after injuries, and knowing that bodies and spirits can't be separated.

My friend and colleague, Fabien Bassett, who generously shared his time and equipment so I could reap the benefits of hypoxia training.

My friends, Penny Cofield, Isabel Cumby, Diane Rendell, and Eva Musseau, who delivered food to keep me fueled in the long hours of training.

My friend and filmmaker, Greg Rainoff, for braving January in St. John's to capture the story of Everest-007, especially how much I had to eat.

Moh Hardin, for shaping my Buddhist path and giving me teachings that I use during every climb and every day.

My sangha, for walking the path with me and sharing its support and care along the journey.

My friends, Colin and Mavis Higgs, for always being there when I need perspective, wine glasses, or a visit to Tim Hortons or Tim's Lake.

My friend and new boss, Mary Bluechardt, for great hugs and understanding.

My friend and colleague, Vera Mitchell, for outfitting me in protective and healing stones.

My friend and photographic mentor, Matt Downey, for his unceasing belief in me and always being a few steps ahead on the mountain reaching his hand down.

My friends, Leslie Grattan and Tony Pierce, for their amazing generosity at just the right moments.

My friends and early writing mentors, Brenda Jackson and Jean Marcel Duciaume, for your unfaltering support of my transition into early adulthood, your skillful coaching of my writing, and the Leysin cookie team.

My editor, Ed Kavanagh, for helping me take a rough stone and polishing it until it was smooth and shiny.

Donna Francis for her belief in this book and hard work in bringing it into fruition.

Steve Bartlett, Jeff Gilhooly, Debbie Cooper, Ann Budgell, and all the other members of the Newfoundland media who helped bring the story of Everest-007 into the public eye (and ears).

Sharon Stoodley for introducing me to Flat Stanley. He was a wonderful traveling companion and he helped me reach out to many children.

My sponsors and supporters, Mountain Equipment Co-op, Good Life Fitness Centres, Arthur James Clothing, The Outfitters, Lowe Alpine, and Columbia Sportswear, for their financial and/or equipment support. I appreciate the time and effort it took to help me out.

My friends, Joanne Coleman, Linda Bartlett, Eric Cumby, and Ron Boland for helping me reach out to potential sponsors.

Phil Ershler, for his wisdom, advice, and words of encouragement.

Paul Adler, for his patient mentoring of my communications technology for the mountain. I couldn't have shared the expedition with the world without his assistance.

My friends, Kristen Zbornic, Margaret Barron, Norm Fair, Natelle Tulk, Jen Lokash, Natalie Beausoleil, Marie Wall, Maureen Dunne, Allison Stringer, Jennifer Mactavish, Zoe Raemer, Leslie Appling, Dory Sample, Laurie Clausen, Sylvia Dresser, and Jean Funk, for being there over years or decades, through mountains and mole hills, and during both inner and outer adventures.

My public school teachers, Mr. Hamilton, Mrs. Woycenko, Ms. Lecky, Mr. Walton, and Mr. Boyko, for nurturing my body, mind, and spirit and giving me lots of room and opportunity to grow.

My supporters, for making contributions of all kinds to Everest-007: Allison Sturge, Andy St John, Ann Chafe, Bev Winsor, Bill Morrissey, Bill Redden, Boyce Taylor, Brenda Galway, Cathy Walsh, Cynde Grieve, Dale Foster, Dan Miller, Darrell Cole, David Thompson, Debbie Godden, Debbie

McGee, Deb Shortal, Denise Hennebury, Denise Hurley, Diane Rendell, Ellen Picard, Ellen Winarskyk, Heather Courage, Jan Cressman, Joan Hawkins, Karen Hertzberg, Karen Ulendorf, Kathleen Winter, Kathy Dwyer, Ken O'Brien, Kevin Redmond, Lee Meehan, Lynn Steinkamp, Mac Gervan, Mark Nutio, Marlene Kavanagh, Michelle Healey, Mike Packard, Moyra Buchan, Muggs Tibbo, Nicole Squires, Nolan White, Pat Hartman, Paul Rose, Peggy Pope, Penny Delong, Peter Noel, Phil Alcock, Russ and Michelle Adams, Randy Coish, Sandra Stavio, Sharon Kaye, Susan Doyle, Susan Sherk, Suzanne Steele, TA's AppleCore Hockey Teammates, Tashia Batstone, Tom Wilkinson, Toni Ryan, and Trudy Veitch.

These schools and organizations, for making contributions to Everest-007: Addictions and Mental Health–Central Health, Baltimore School, Becoming an Outdoors Woman, Beechy Cove Elementary School, Body, Mind and Spirit Retreats, Boys and Girls Club, Clarenville Rotary Club, College of the North Atlantic, Community Youth Network, Cowan Heights Elementary School, Eastern Health, Edge Diving Club, Exploits Valley Community Coalition, Fatima Academy, Fortis Properties, Genesis Centre, Good Karma Knits, Hazelwood Elementary School, Holy Cross School, Holy Heart of Mary High School, Holy Trinity Elementary School, Leary's Brook Junior High School, Leysin American School, MacDonald Drive Junior High, Macpherson School, MADD-Central Chapter, Mary Queen of Peace School, Newfoundland Certified General Accountants Association, Newfoundland & Labrador Employee Assistance Program Association, Newfoundland School for the Deaf, Safety Newfoundland and Labrador, Positive Thinkers Club, Saint Francis of Assisi School, Shad Valley Program, St. Anne's School, St. Bernard's Elementary School, St. Edward's School, St. John's Home School Support Group, St. Kevin's School, St. Matthew's School, St. Peter's Elementary School, St. Thomas Pathfinders Group, Status of Women Central, Stella Maris Academy, The Central West Committee Against Violence, Town of Bishop's Falls, Town of Grand Falls-Windsor, Women in Technology and Trades Program, and Woodland Primary School.

And finally, my cyber support team, for always being there to receive my words week after week and sending inspiration whenever I needed it. And specifically, for these folks who followed the expedition closely and sent regular messages of encouragement, Fiona, MC, Scott, Ken.nz, Limerick Queen, WM Popper, Ann and Graham, Shelagh, Andrea, Lorraine, Shepp, Liselle, Shelley, Sandra, Shanda, Jill, Nancy and Erika.

GLOSSARY

ACCLIMATIZATION
The process of adapting to higher elevations and adjusting to the lower oxygen content in the air as one climbs a mountain.

ACONCAGUA
The tallest mountain in the Western Hemisphere at 6,962 metres or 22,841 feet. Located in Argentina it is part of the Andes Mountain Range. It is one of the Seven Summits.

ACUTE MOUNTAIN SICKNESS (AMS)
A form of illness brought on by prolonged exposure to high altitude. Some of the symptoms include headaches, nausea, fatigue, light-headedness, water retention, and insomnia.

ANDES
A mountain range located in South America.

ANNAPURNA CIRCUIT
A three-week trek in Nepal that circumnavigates the Annapurna massifs.

ARNICA
A type of mountain plant belonging to the sunflower family often used in herbal medicine to treat bruising and swelling.

ASCENDER
A climbing tool used to ascend ropes and to prevent falls. When attached to a rope, an ascender will slide up the rope freely but grips the rope when downward force is applied preventing the ascender from moving backwards.

BANDY
A winter sport, played in Northern Europe, that is often considered a predecessor of ice hockey.

BASE CAMP
The camp from which a mountaineering expedition begins its climb, often acting as a main base of operations.

BASE CAMP TROTS
Refers to the diarrhea that many climbers experience while living at the base
camp of Mount Everest.

BODHISATTVA
"Awake being." A bodhisattva is someone who has become enlightened or
who inspires to enlightenment and has dedicated his or her life to liberating
all sentient beings.

BODHISATTVA VOW
The Bodhisattva Vow is taken after the Refuge Vow. Someone taking the
Bodhisattva Vow declares that she or he will not realize enlightenment until
all sentient beings have done so and dedicates her or his practice to helping
others attain enlightenment.

BUTTER LAMPS
Small lamps that burn yak butter or vegetable oil and are commonly found
in Tibetan Buddhist temples.

CABOT TOWER
A tower located at the top of Signal Hill, in St John's, Newfoundland and
Labrador, Canada. The tower was built in 1897 to celebrate Queen Victoria's
Diamond Jubilee and the 400th anniversary of John Cabot's discovery of
Newfoundland and Labrador.

CACHE
A quantity of gear, food or fuel that a climbing expedition buries or stores
in the snow or ground for retrieval at a later time.

CAPE SPEAR
The most easterly point in North America, located just south of St. John's,
Newfoundland and Labrador, Canada.

CARABINER
A metal loop with a spring loaded gate, used by climbers to attach safety
harnesses to climbing ropes.

CARSTENSZ PYRAMID
The tallest mountain in the Australian continent at 4,884 metres or 16,024 feet. It is located in Indonesia and is part of the Sudirman Mountain Range. The mountain is also known as Puncak Jaya. It is one of the Seven Summits.

CBC
Canadian Broadcasting Corporation.

CHANG
A form of barley beer.

CHOMOLUNGMA
See Mount Everest.

CHO OYU
The sixth highest mountain in the world at 8,201 metres or 26,906 feet, located in the Himalayan Mountain Range about twenty kilometres west of Mount Everest.

CHORTEN
A type of Buddhist monument or temple that symbolizes the elements of water, sky, fire, space, and earth.

COL
A narrow mountain pass sometimes referred to as a saddle.

CRAMPONS
Metal spikes that can be affixed to a climber's boots to provide them with traction on snow and ice. Crampons allow climbers to climb steep or icy slopes.

CRAMPON TECHNIQUES
Refers to different methods for using crampons to traverse different terrain.

CREVASSE
A break or crack in a glacier, which results form the gradual melting and movement of the glacier. Crevasses can range in size from a just a few centimeters to many metres in width and can be hundreds of metres deep. Crevasses are very dangerous as they can often be covered by snow (known as a snow bridge) making them very hard to detect.

DHARMA
The teachings of the Buddha.

DENALI
The tallest mountain in North America at 6,193 metres or 20,320 feet. The mountain is part of the Alaskan Mountain Range and is located north-north-west of Anchorage, Alaska. It is also known as Mount McKinley. It is one of the Seven Summits.

EAST COAST TRAIL
A 540 kilometre hiking trail located on the east coast of Newfoundland and Labrador, Canada.

ELBRUS
The tallest mountain in Europe at 5,642 metres or 18,510 feet. It is located in the Western Caucasus Mountains in Russia near the boarder of Georgia. It is one of the Seven Summits.

EL VIENTO BLANCO
Sudden wind storms associated with Aconcagua.

FIXED LINES
Climbing lines that are affixed to a mountain to provide a margin of safety in case a climber falls.

FOG DEVILS
A Quebec Major Junior Hockey League team based in St John's, Newfoundland and Labrador, Canada.

GIARDIA
A parasite that grows and reproduces in the small intestine causing Giardiasis, also known as "Beaver Fever." Symptoms include fever, stomach cramps, loss of appetite, diarrhea, upset stomach and vomiting.

GO2ALTITUDE
A device that reduces the percentage of oxygen in the air mimicking increases in altitude, which allows individuals to train as if they were at a higher elevation.

GORAK SHEP
A frozen lakebed located on the route to Mount Everest South Col Base Camp. It is often the last camp that expeditions overnight at before arriving in base camp.

GLACIER
A large slow moving mass of ice often located on a mountain slope.

GLACIER TRAVEL
Techniques used to travel on a glacier often requiring climbers to tie onto a rope to form a rope team.

GRAVOL
A drug used to treat nausea and motion sickness. It is also known as Dramamine.

GU
A high-energy food product, basically flavored corn syrup, packaged in a squeezable container that is easy to consume quickly in cold, harsh conditions.

GUGLIELMO MARCONI
An Italian inventor who pioneered work with the radiotelegraph. He and his team received the first transatlantic wireless transmission in 1901, when a Morse code message from Cornwall, England was received in St. John's, Newfoundland and Labrador, Canada.

HARNESS
A safety device that fastens around the waist of a climber and is then attached to a climbing rope.

HEADLAMP
A small flashlight attached to a strap that allows a climber to wear the light on their head thus keeping their hands free.

HIGH ALTITUDE CEREBRAL EDEMA (HACE)
A potentially lethal high altitude illness caused by brain swelling. It causes severe headache, changes in mental status and difficulty walking.

HIGH ALTITUDE PULMONARY EDEMA (HAPE)
A potentially lethal high altitude illness caused by leakage of fluid into the
lungs. It causes difficulty breathing, fatigue, and weakness.

HIMALAYAS
A mountain range in Asia.

HYPOXIA
Refers to having a lack of oxygen reach the vital organs or the oxygen dep-
rivation that a climber experiences at altitude.

HYPOXIC TRAINING
To train in a hypoxic state.

ICE AXE
A climbing tool shaped much like a small pickaxe with an adze at one end
and a point at the other. It is used for self-arrest, balance, griping ice, and
cutting snow.

INTERNATIONAL MOUNTAIN GUIDES (IMG)
An international mountaineering outfitter with its headquarters located in
Washington State, USA.

INUKSHUK
A sculpted pile of rocks used as a milestone or directional marker by the
Inuit people of Canada to navigate terrain in the far north.

KATAS
Ceremonial scarves often made of white or cream colored silk that are presented to individuals leaving on a trip as a sign of honor and respect.

KHUMBU COUGH
A term that refers to the cough many climbers developed while at Everest
Base Camp due to the thin air, it is named after the Khumbu Glacier.

KHUMBU ICEFALL
A steep, dangerous section of the Khumbu Glacier characterized by huge
unstable seracs and crevasses located adjacent to Mount Everest base camp
on the Nepal side of the mountain.

KILIMANJARO
The tallest mountain in Africa at 5,895 metres or 19,341 feet. It is located in north-eastern Tanzania. It is one of the Seven Summits.

LADDER CROSSING
Refers to the use of metal ladders to cross crevasses in the Khumbu Icefall. Often several ladders must be joined together to span a crevasse. Such crossings are often done while wearing crampons, which can make walking on the ladder very challenging.

LAMA
The head monk of a Tibetan Buddhist monastery.

LHASANG
A Buddhist purification ceremony in which juniper is burned.

LHOTSE
The forth-highest mountain in the world at 8,515 metres or 27,940 feet. It is located in the Himalayan Mountain Range and is connected to Mount Everest by the South Col.

LHOTSE FACE
The western side of Lhotse.

MALA
A string of beads used to keep track of the number of mantras said.

MANI STONES
Small rocks or pebbles inscribed with a mantra often in the form of a Buddhist prayer.

MANI WALLS
Walls which contain mani stones.

MANTRA
A religious poem or prayer, often recited seven, twenty-one, or one-hundred and eight times.

MAOIST
Refers to the Communist Party of Nepal.

MEMORIAL UNIVERSITY OF NEWFOUNDLAND (MUN)
The largest comprehensive university in Atlantic Canada located primarily in St John's, Newfoundland and Labrador, Canada. The university is also known as Memorial.

MORAINE
An accumulation of boulders, stones, or other debris carried and deposited by a glacier.

MOUNT EVEREST
The tallest mountain in Asia and in the world at 8,850 metres or 29,029 feet. Part of the Himalayan Mountain Range it is located on the boarder between Nepal and Tibet (China). It is also know as Chomolungma, Qomolangma and Sagarmatha. It is one of the Seven Summits.

MOUNT LOGAN
The tallest mountain in Canada and the second tallest mountain in North America at 5,959 metres or 19,551 feet, it is located in the Yukon Territory.

MOUNT MCKINLEY
See Denali.

NECK GAITER
A type of round scarf.

NEWFOUNDLAND AND LABRADOR
The most easterly province in Canada.

NEWFOUNDLAND TRICOLOR FLAG
This refers to the pink, white and green flag of the old Newfoundland republic.

NTV
A local television channel located in St John's, Newfoundland and Labrador, Canada.

O2 SATURATION
A measure of the percentage of oxygen in the blood that indicates the status of one's acclimatization.

PENTITENTES
Ice formations much like upside down icicles.

POTALA PALACE
Located in Lhasa, Tibet, the Potala Palace was the chief residence of the Dalai Lama.

PRAYER WHEELS
A cylinder or wheel often made of wood, metal or some other rigid material that is positioned on a spindle. Encased within the wheel, are Buddhist prayers or mantras. Spinning the wheel is believed to have the same effect as orally reciting the prayer.

PROSTRATIONS
Posing the body in a prone position used to show reverence and gain merit.

PUJA CEREMONY
A Sherpa ceremony of offering to the mountain gods often performed at base camp, before an expedition begins climbing.

PUJA ALTER
A stone alter used in a puja ceremony.

QUINZHEE
A snow hut, originally made by Aboriginal People of the Canadian plains, by piling up snow into a mound, letting it settle, and then digging out the center to form a concave shelter.

RAPPELLING
To descend steep terrain by sliding down a rope attached to the climber's harness.

REFUGE CEREMONY
A ceremony during which a person takes the Refuge Vow. In taking the Refuge Vow, a person becomes a Buddhist by taking refuge in the Buddha, the Dharma, and the Sangha.

RING OF FIRE CHALLENGES
Mental and physical challenges TA undertook as part of her training to climb Mount Everest.

RUM DOODLE
Refers to an imaginary mountain that is 40,000.5 feet high and a Kathmandu restaurant icon.

SAGARMATHA
See Mount Everest.

SANGHA
A community of people who have taken the Refuge Vow and/or who follow the teachings of the Buddha.

SERAC
A large pointed mass of ice in a glacier isolated by intersecting crevasses or by an icefall.

SEVEN SUMMITS
Refers to the highest mountains on each of the seven continents. The mountains are: Mount Everest, Aconcagua, Denali, Elbrus, Kilimanjaro, Vinson Massif, and Carstensz Pyramid. Some climbers also include Kosciuszko in the Seven Summits list, as it is the highest peak on the mainland of Australia.

SHERPA
An ethnic group of people originating in the mountainous regions of Nepal and Tibet. The term sherpa can also refer to the job of sherpa which involves working for climbing expeditions and often includes tasks such as carrying goods, fixing ropes, establishing routes, setting up camp and rescuing climbers. Due to their ability to function at high altitude, many Sherpa people also work as sherpas and have become indispensable associates to climbing expeditions.

SHERPANI
A female Sherpa.

SIGNAL HILL
A large hill that overlooks the city of St John's, Newfoundland and Labrador, Canada. The first transatlantic wireless transmission was received at this location in 1901 by Guglielmo Marconi.

SOBEY'S
A large grocery store chain in Canada.

SOUTH COL
Refers to the col located between Lhoste and Mount Everest. It also refers to one of the two main climbing routes for expeditions attempting to climb Mount Everest.

SPINDRIFT
Clouds of blowing snow.

STUPA
A type of Buddhist structure or building shaped like a dome or mound often containing the relics of an enlightened being.

SUMMIT
The highest point on a mountain.

TELY TEN
An annual 10-mile running race held in St John's, Newfoundland and Labrador, Canada.

TOUTS
People who solicit goods or businesses in a persistent or urgent manner.

TSAMPA
A type of barley flour that is a staple of the Sherpa diet.

TIBETAN PRAYER FLAGS (PRAYER FLAGS)
Colorful pieces of cloth with Buddhist prayers printed on them, often found strung along mountain ridges and peaks to bless the surrounding area.

TIM HORTONS
An international restaurant chain that specializes in coffee and doughnuts,
founded in 1964 in Hamilton, Ontario, Canada and named after the famous
hockey player, Tim Horton.

TIBETAN PLATEAU
A large plateau located in East Asia, on which most of the autonomous
region of Tibet is located.

TONGLEN
The Buddhist practice of breathing in and taking the suffering of self and
others and breathing out and sending relief for that suffering.

VINSON MASSIF
The tallest mountain in Antarctica at 4,892 metres or 16,050 feet. It is part
of the Sentential Range in the Ellsworth Mountains. It is one of the Seven
Summits.

VO2 MAX
Refers to the maximum capacity of the human body to transfer and use oxygen.

WESTERN CWM
A broad glacial valley that ends at the base of the Lhotse Face that must be
traversed by Everest climbers using the south col route.

ZOPKIOS
A hybrid animal that is the offspring of a cow and a yak. They are often
used to carry supplies in high altitude regions of Nepal and Tibet.

AUTHOR BIOGRAPHY

Dr. TA Loeffler brings 20 years of expertise leading people through significant life-changing experiences to every facet of her work. Her work and adventures have taken her to 35 different countries and five different continents. As a Professor of Outdoor Recreation at Memorial University of Newfoundland, TA has developed a reputation for excellence in experiential education because her students are more likely to be outside chasing icebergs than sitting in a classroom. TA is attempting to complete "The Seven Summits," the highest peak on all seven continents.

TA believes that we all long for a balanced, engaged, and creative life that challenges us to be the best we can possibly be. She models this belief in her life on a daily basis and combines her broad range of skills to inspire all to create the life they truly want. With compassion, care, presence, and playfulness, TA creates a safe space for all to learn and grow within. Using her vast collection of outdoor adventures to create metaphors that provide new ways to see and transform the inevitable obstacles of life, TA's multi-media presentations inform, educate, inspire, and motivate. As a filmmaker and motivational speaker, TA understands the power of metaphor to initiate and sustain life change. TA inspires hope, possibility, and vision in those whose lives she touches.

TA has received international and national recognition for her innovative teaching and motivational speaking. In 2006, The Globe and Mail named TA, "A Class Act" and she received the Association of Atlantic Universities Distinguished Teaching Award. The Canadian Association for the Advancement of Women in Sport named TA to their 2006 Top Twenty Most Influential Women in Canadian Sport and Physical Activity List. Additionally, TA received the Memorial University President's Award for Distinguished Teaching in 2005 and the Association for Experiential Education named TA the Outstanding Experiential Teacher of the Year in 1999. In 2007, the Association for Experiential Education presented TA with the Karl Rhonke Creativity Award.

During her recent climb on Mount Everest, TA updated her website daily from 21,000 feet above sea level using a personal digital assistant and satellite phone. During the year leading up to Everest, TA spread her message of "Big Dreams, Big Goals" to over 10,000 youth in the province of Newfoundland and Labrador. Having heard TA speak, many of these same children followed her climb via the web and sent supportive messages to her on the mountain via email and yak mail.

TA is a talented athlete. She uses strength training, running, biking, yoga, cycling and step aerobics to prepare for her expeditions. She has a passion for hockey and has played every position on the ice including goaltender. TA has coached several championship winning hockey teams and has officiated at the national championship level. Through her experience in both sports and outdoor adventure, TA intimately appreciates teamwork and knows how to bring teams together to accomplish their goals and fulfill their greatest potential.

For more of TA's adventures, please visit www.taloeffler.com